Texas Treasure

Billy Kenon and the Padre Island Shipwrecks of 1554

by

Dr. Robert H. Baer

Texas Treasure

Published by:
Signum Ops, 435 Nora Ave., Merritt Island, FL 32952

ISBN 9781652795575
Library of Congress Catalog-in-Publication data:
Baer, Robert H.
Texas Treasure

First Printed Edition, March , 2020

Graphics & Cover by:
T. L. Armstrong

All photos provided by Billy Kenon unless otherwise noted.

Captain Billy Kenon
Dedicates This Book To

His Wife & Partner

Esther Kaevando Kenon

And His Attorneys & Friends

Jack Sanchez
1945 - 1987
&
Dennis Sanchez

My interest and initiation into the story of the Padre Island shipwrecks of 1554 began in the early 1990s when I was the Compliance Archaeologist for a salvage company named Jupiter Wreck Incorporated (JWI) that was headquartered in Jupiter, Florida, a small 'upscale beachfront community' located at the northern extreme of Palm Beach County, Florida. The Jupiter Wreck team was engaged in the excavation of what was later documented to be the remains of a seventeenth-century shipwreck, the *San Miguel de Archangel* lost in 1659. As the compliance archaeologist for the project I had several responsibilities; first I was responsible for the routine paperwork that JWI was responsible for submitting to the State of Florida. This consisted of daily worksheets that recorded the position of the salvage vessels when excavating, and what treasure or artifact material was recovered from a particular excavation site. My second responsibility was to carry out an archaeological interpretation of the scattered shipwreck site that lay just south of the Jupiter Inlet consisting of ten cannon, two anchors, and thousands of coins and artifacts that lay strewn over several acres of nearshore seafloor in water that averaged a depth of twenty-five feet.

The Jupiter Wreck story was like many treasure hunting sagas, one of the original partners, Peter Leo, had discovered wreckage of an historic shipwreck consisting of exposed cannons and anchors lying in the nearshore shallows south of Jupiter Inlet. He then approached a local businessman named Dominic Addario, who agreed to form a partnership and then attempt to salvage the shipwreck. Together, the three partners, Dominic Addario, Peter Leo, and Earl Young, retained an admiralty attorney and filed for salvage in the U.S. Federal Court. Eventually, pursuant to court action, the State of Florida and JWI reached an agreement that led to JWI being awarded salvage rights to the site. Under the terms of the agreement, the State of Florida would receive all one-of-a-kind artifacts of historic and cultural importance, and twenty percent of the salvaged treasure — gold and silver coins and bullion. The remainder of the shipwreck treasure accrued to the JWI partners and their investors.

My first personal encounter with Billy Kenon was at the *San Miguel de Archangel* site where Billy was working as a sub-contractor aboard his seventy-five-foot salvage vessel the *Mr. Wizard*, a converted shrimper workboat that was capable of excavating a twenty-foot trench in seventy feet of water. I immediately liked Billy and his crew, and after Kenon left Jupiter with his share of the season's treasure, I began to follow other Kenon salvage projects including several nineteenth-century shipwrecks off the coast of South Carolina.

Sometime later I delved deeper into Billy Kenon's background as a treasure hunter and learned that Billy along with several associates in the early 1960s had formed a salvage corporation named the Platoro Group with the intent of searching for shipwreck sites just north of Port Mansfield Channel on Padre Island, Texas. My interest was immediately aroused! I had previously read two books that documented the archaeology of what would come to be known as the Padre Island Shipwrecks of 1554. These two books were titled, *The Nautical Archaeology of Padre Island*, by J. Barto Arnold and Robert S. Weddle, and *Texas, Legacy From the Gulf* by Doris Olds, of the Texas Museum at Austin. To be candid, both of the books, Arnold and Weddle, as well as Olds, were dismissive of the several years of fieldwork that had been carried out by the Platoro Group, when in fact, Platoro had recovered most of the important shipwreck artifacts and treasure that now reside in the State of Texas collection in Austin, and shared in other exhibition venues as well.

At first, Billy was reluctant to discuss the case; as it turned out the State of Texas confiscated all of the treasure recovered by Billy and his colleagues, although a financial settlement was eventually worked out between the Texas cultural authorities and Platoro. Soon Billy and

I slipped into an easy conservation and I became acutely interested in exactly what had occurred on Padre Island, both historically, over the course of the salvage, and during the acrimonious litigation that followed. As stated, the two official histories were dismissive of Platoro and one of the few names that appeared were the Znika brothers, from Gary, Indiana who had initiated the salvage operation, and who had recruited Billy Kenon as the project field manager. The only 'popular book' that discussed the Padre Island shipwrecks and the Platoro group was, *The Treasure Divers Guide* by John Potter. Potter had traveled to Padre Island at the same time that Billy Kenon was directing field operations at the shipwreck site. Kenon is vehement in his opinion that the Potter received his information from second hand and biased sources; this controversy is examined later in this book.

After I began to investigate the Padre Island shipwreck story I found the Potter version to indeed be in error. At this point, I decided to tell the complete Padre Island story. It would be difficult after some fifty years had passed, many of the principal players were deceased, and the treasure hunter records were scattered. The two books cited above were helpful but their content motivated me to look for other resources which came to include hundreds of newspaper articles and legal documents generated by John O. Stiles, the Platoro attorney, as well as Commissioner Jerry Sadler, the State of Texas Land Commissioner, who had led the movement to confiscate the Platoro treasure.

Thankfully, Billy Kenon had kept most of the court records, the administrative correspondence between the Platoro Group principals, as well as numerous newspaper accounts of what I began to refer to as the Padre Island Treasure Saga. The sad aspect of the Platoro Group salvage at Padre Island was the fact that outside of a small suitcase full of documents, and faded newspaper clippings, the truth was that Platoro and Billy Kenon had no real lasting voice in the history of the Padre Island shipwreck salvage; the story had been usurped by Arnold, Weddle and the State of Texas legal and administrative bureaucracy.

Much of this Padre Island Shipwreck story describes the administrative and court battle that evolved over some twenty-five years as Billy Kenon fought in the Texas Courts to acquire a fair share of the treasure and artifacts that he believed rightfully belonged to Platoro. As this book describes, at the same time that Platoro was battling the

State of Texas in State and Federal Courts, the State of Florida cultural resource officials had been brought into an uneasy truce with the treasure hunter community that remains in place to this day. The Florida treasure salvage program had begun in the early 1960s about the same time as Kenon and the Platoro Group discovered the remains of the lost Spanish 1554 vessels in the shallows off Padre Island. While not popular within the wider cultural and academic community, the Florida treasure salvage program has added immeasurably to the archaeological and historical record.

More follows in this book describing the intertwined legacy of shipwreck archaeology and shipwreck salvage. It is safe to say that the animosities between the archaeology and salvage community will never be healed. It is, however, an irrevocable truth that without the regulated treasure salvage industry little of the world's shipwreck and maritime history would be known today!

In Florida the administrative program designated how the treasure would be divided, and what archaeological oversight would be required in the field. Carl Clausen, who appears later in the Padre Island saga, pioneered the role of the archaeologist working in the field with treasure hunters and was the first State of Florida Underwater Archaeologist. After moving on from Florida, perhaps looking for a new challenge, Clausen reappeared in Texas in the same capacity. In the early days, the State of Florida required that each boat licensed to treasure hunt would have a State Field Agent on board to monitor the fieldwork, and document the artifacts and treasure, as they came aboard; this is no longer done! The State of Florida was also responsible for the conservation of the treasure and the maintenance of the field reports and records and maintains these records in the state capital today. Although much maligned by the conservative archaeological community, the treasure hunters in Florida have contributed substantially to the state's shipwreck heritage. A number of popular books have been written by treasure hunters who salvaged the Spanish 1622, 1715, and 1733 shipwrecks. One of the most popular and adventure-filled books is *The Rainbow Chasers* by T.L. Armstrong and Tommy Gore. *The Rainbow Chasers* is an informal history of the 1715 salvage program from the perspective of a treasure hunter and a state regulator — an informative read! Also, two shipwreck museums have been established in Florida both by the Mel Fisher Treasure Salvors organization; the museums are respectively located in Key West, Florida near the 1622 shipwreck sites, and the other in Sebastian, Florida near the sites of the 1715 shipwrecks.

Another theme that runs through this book is the controversy that surrounds commercial treasure hunting. Simply stated the archaeological community views treasure hunting as 'beyond the pale', where the motives of the treasure hunters are inimical to any acceptable standards of scientific inquiry and methodology. Truth be told it has been the courts that have forced treasure hunters to work with archaeologists; as I stated earlier, a requirement at the Jupiter Shipwreck Site was that a certified professional archaeologist be retained by the salvage company to conduct research as far the physical limitations of the site would allow. One of my contributions to Florida history and shipwreck archaeology was a book titled, *The Last Voyage of the San Miguel De Archangel*. This monograph was researched utilizing many diverse resources, as is this study of the Padre Island shipwrecks. More importantly, both the Jupiter and the Padre Island studies tell the personal story of the treasure hunters and their associates along with the important social and cultural background that constitutes a modern shipwreck salvage project.

As this book was in development, I visited a used book store where I spotted a large 'coffee table' sized book on the shelf. It was titled, *The History of Shipwrecks* by Angus Konstam. I took the book off the shelf. It was so clean and crisp, it looked like it had been published yesterday, but no, the book had a publication date of 1999, some 21 years ago. Opening it, I was struck by the great color illustrations and photographs of very good quality. The text itself was the obligatory thumbnail sketch of ships as diverse as the Greek Classical Period, Kyrenia shipwreck, and the *U.S.S. Monitor* of Civil War fame. Thumbing through the book, 'lo and behold', there it was... the Padre Island wrecks! All the shipwreck profiles were no more than two pages with a few color illustrations; the Padre Island article had an anchor lying on a bed of ballast stones, one of the wrought-iron cannon, a bombardeta, and a portion of the preserved hull of the *San Esteban*. I scanned the article for personal names! There was J. Barto Arnold, the State of Texas archaeologist...reading on I found the name "Platoro" and "seventeen-year lawsuit"; that was it! Of the work performed by the treasure hunters and their archaeologist, Mendel Peterson of the Smithsonian Institution there was nothing!

Finally a few words on the historical context of the Padre Island shipwreck salvage. Historically speaking the Padre Island salvage performed by Billy Kenon and his associates from the Platoro Group must be considered in the setting of its time, the early Colonial History of the Spanish Conquest of the Americas. The loss of the three Spanish vessels offshore of Padre Island occurred a mere fifty years after the end of the Christopher Columbus era in the New World. Thus the story of Billy Kenon and Platoro is intertwined in the early colonial history of the Americas. The Platoro story could not have been told and would have no meaning without the wider context of the Spanish seaborne treasure trade, the dynamics of the shipwrecks as they occurred off of Padre Island, and then the tragedy of the survivor's forced-march while attempting to reach safety in Mexico. It is also important to compare the work by the State of Texas archaeology teams that assumed the responsibility of the shipwreck fieldwork after Platoro was enjoined from future excavation at the site. Lastly, a discussion of the treasure and shipwreck artifacts has been made to reinforce the cultural importance of the Padre Island shipwreck project and to set the record straight.

The Fleet

The story of the Padre Island shipwrecks begins in the middle of the sixteenth century. In 1552 a fleet of 54 ships sailed from the Spanish port of Sanlucar de Barrameda, Spain to the New World under the command of Captain-General Bartolome Carreno. After leaving Spain the Carreno fleet sailed southwest to the Canary Islands, then due west to the Americas. After a voyage of approximately one month, the fleet arrived in the Greater Antilles port of Santo Domingo, on the Island of Hispaniola. After disembarking passengers and cargo the fleet would sail on to Havana, then separate into two separate fleets, one sailing south through the Caribbean to the Isthmus of Panama, the other sailing into the Gulf of Mexico along the Yucatan coast of

A lanteen-rigged vessel of the mid-16th-century
Illustration: Dan Wukits

Mexico, destined for the port of Vera Cruz. Two years later in 1554, on their return voyage from Vera Cruz to Spain, three of the original 1552 vessels, the *San Esteban, Espiritu Santo* and the *Santa Maria de Yciar* were lost along the present Texas coast off Padre Island just north of Port Mansfield Channel.

Spanish fleets performed two basic missions; the outward bound fleet from Spain to the Americas transported European goods and passengers to the Spanish Colonial Empire; then some months later they returned to Spain with the gold and silver treasure that had been mined and refined in Spain's possessions in South America and Mexico. The Spanish treasure fleets generally sailed on a yearly basis, a fleet out to the Americas, and a return fleet home to Spain. The largest and most well-known treasure vessels were the galleons, large triple decked vessels with three masts that had the largest cargo-carrying capacity. Smaller cargo vessels, the 'naos' had a significantly smaller transport capacity than a galleon, however, these vessels were the workhorses of trans-Atlantic trade.

Three of the vessels that made the outward voyage from Spain subsequently lost off Padre Island in 1554, were the *San Esteban*, the *Espiritu Santo*, and the *Santa Maria de Yciar*. The *San Esteban*, although not a galleon, was the largest of the three vessels. Her captain, Francisco Del Huerto, had a well-established record as a ship's captain having made several voyages to the New World, to South America and Central America; there is no record of his sailing to Mexico (New Spain) and the port of Vera Cruz. The next largest vessel was the *Espiritu Santo*. Her captain was Damian Martin who had previously voyaged to the Americas but had not sailed the Gulf of Mexico. The smallest vessel was the *Santa Maria de Yciar*. Her master, Alonso Ojos, was the least experienced of the three captains; however, her owner, Miguel de Jauregui, sailed with the vessel as a passenger and had previous experience as a captain and pilot. Jauregui was the most experienced of all the ship's captains, having made at least ten round trip voyages to the New World, and at least three voyages to New Spain and the port of Vera Cruz.

However, it was a mixed fleet, with the three above-cited vessels judged as seaworthy. The majority of the vessels in the outward bound fleet were in poor condition, having reached the end of their life as dependable cargo vessels. After a long voyage beset by storms, unseasonable contrary winds, and attacks by pirates and privateers the fleet eventually reached the Caribbean. The fleet then divided into two smaller fleets, and sailed on to their final destinations, eventually to take on massive treasure cargoes in Panama, and Vera Cruz, Mexico, then returning with this New World wealth to Spain. From the 16th through the 18th centuries these fleets fed the insatiable need of the Spanish monarchy for the wealth of the Americas. This insatiable need for gold and silver forced the Spanish monarchy to consummate alliances through marriage, fight wars, and also fund the expensive day-to-day activities of their own royal household.

Port Isabel Texas – Beginnings

In 1959, a nineteen-year-old boat captain from Port Isabel, Texas named Billy Kenon began to hear stories about Spanish colonial coins, "Pieces of Eight" that were found on the beach at the mouth of the Port Mansfield Channel that led from the Gulf of Mexico into Laguna Madre, a body of water separating Padre Island from the Texas mainland. Padre Island is the longest, undeveloped, government-protected barrier island in the United States, stretching some one hundred miles along the Texas gulf coast from Corpus Christi to the Rio Grande River. The island has a long history, first as a Spanish possession during the Age of Exploration, then during the early 'Texas Republic', and later 'Early Statehood Period' when the island supported a unique and thriving cattle industry. Spanish Colonial archives documented the Tristan de Luna expedition to the area as well as tales of a small Spanish treasure fleet that was lost some-where along the Texas coast in 1554.

Billy Kenon was born in St. Augustine, Florida in 1941. Spending his childhood in America's oldest city Billy roamed the streets that were still in a sense unspoiled and not yet inundated with the influx of tourists that crowded the city with the coming of the later intrastate highway system. Billy remembered that on some weekdays he had the fortress, Castillo De San Marcos nearly to himself, and came to know the fortress as well as he knew his own home in west St. Augustine. Billy's dad William Kenon Sr., was a shrimper by profession and oper-ated shrimp boats out of St. Augustine as well as at Fernandina, a fish-ing community thirty miles north of St. Augustine near Jacksonville. Just after World War II, in 1949, Bill Kenon decided to move the family shrimping business from the oldest U.S. City founded in 1565 by the Spanish conquistador Pedro Menendez de Aviles, to the shrimp-rich waters of the Gulf of Mexico and relocated to Morgan City, Louisiana. Eventually, the family business fishing for 'pink gold', prospered to the point where another shrimping business was established at the bor-der town of Brownsville, Texas. Moving again the family located to Raymondville Texas, near the city of Port Mansfield across Laguna Madre from Padre Island.

As a teenager Billy worked in the family business, then began to branch out on his own, eventually buying a surplus U.S. Navy LSM ,which is a designation for "landing ship machinery". She was a fifty-foot long vessel that he converted to use in the local salvage industry around Port Mansfield. Billy and the vessel he named *Little Lady* worked at a myriad of jobs from winching grounded shrimp boats out of the Padre Island surf to transporting general cargo around the Port Mansfield and wider gulf coast region.

The Little Lady in the boat yard for maintainance
Photos: Billy Kenon

The Little Lady and another LSM are seen here re-floating
a shrimp boat in Port Mansfield.
Photo: Billy Kenon

Around 1963 as Billy recalls he was working near the north jetties on Padre Island when he saw a jeep driving south down the hard-packed sand beach toward the Port Mansfield ship channel. The driver of the jeep introduced himself as Gus Znika (Za-neeka) from Gary, Indiana. Znika after crossing the causeway from Corpus Christi, had made the adventurous and difficult, one hundred mile drive down the hard-packed sand just above the low tide line to the ship channel because he wanted to visit the spot where treasure coins had been discovered on the beach. Znika told Kenon that he had first learned about the Padre Island treasure finds in "Lost Treasure Magazine" a periodical popular among metal detector, beachcomber hobbyists. As a matter of fact, there was a great deal of interest in the stretch of beach just north of the Port Mansfield channel entrance; so many coins had been found along this roughly three-mile stretch of shoreline that local restaurants featured fanciful Padre Island Treasure maps as place mats.

Kenon was impressed with Znika's pluck and adventurous spirit. Rather than have Znika make the long return trip to Corpus Christi, Billy maneuvered the *Little Lady* up to the beach, lowered the ramp of the landing craft, and transported Znika and the jeep to Port Mansfield where he could make his way back to 'Corpus' on the mainland. While visiting with Billy in Port Mansfield, Znika returned to Padre Island and beachcombed for coins, reportedly finding several. Camping out on the beach and sitting around a campfire, Kenon and Znika discussed the potential of finding shipwrecks that might lie just several hundred yards away, beyond the gentle Padre Island surf. This visit between Kenon and Znika set the course for the future. Znika returned to Indiana and began to contact potential investors and made plans to return to Padre Island.

While Znika was away in Indiana, Billy began to make inquiries around the Port Mansfield area and located a few of the beachcombers that had found the coins along the Padre Island seashore. Several coins he was shown were Spanish and cleaning had revealed that they bore the date 1554. Some of the popular Texas history books that Billy found at the local library contained information indicating that three Spanish treasure galleons sailing from Vera Cruz to Havana in 1554 had been lost somewhere in the Gulf of Mexico, perhaps along the Texas coast. Billy noted the names of these vessels; the *San Esteban,* the *Espiritu Santo,* and the *Santa Maria de Yciar.*

If Spanish treasure ships had been lost in the Gulf in 1554, Billy realized that this was only some sixty years after Columbus' fourth voyage to the New World when the 'Admiral of the Ocean Sea' sailed the south coast of Cuba and the Central American coast from Honduras to the Isthmus of Panama. Billy believed that if Znika was going to form a treasure hunting consortium that the prospective partners better learn all they could about exploration and the gold and silver trade in the Spanish Colonial Period.

The Age of Exploration in the Gulf of Mexico

The Age of Discovery began in the New World with the four voyages of Christopher Columbus that began in 1492, with his voyage from Spain to his first landfall on the island that is now believed to be San Salvador Island in the southeast Bahamas group of islands. In his three additional voyages, Columbus made wide-ranging explorations that included the eastern Bahamas, and the Greater Antilles consisting of the islands of Hispaniola, Puerto Rico, and Cuba. Eventually, on his fourth voyage, Columbus reached the coastline of Central America then sailed south along the Caribbean coast to Venezuela. Columbus died with an inexact understanding of where he had been, or what he had discovered. Only a short sail across the Straits of Florida from Havana and Columbus would have reached the Florida Keys and soon after the mainland of Florida, thus reaching North America. Columbus died believing that he had reached Asia, had he had the time to undertake a fifth voyage of discovery perhaps the intrepid navigator would have reached what the Spanish would come to call "La Florida".

A mere nine years after Columbus' fourth voyage (1502-3), Juan Ponce de Leon the Governor of Puerto Rico set sail to push forward the cartography of the Columbus voyages making two voyages of discovery himself, the first in 1513, and the second in 1521. In 1513, sailing through the Old Bahama Channel that separated Hispaniola and Cuba from the Bahama Islands, Ponce turned north into the conveyor belt current of the Gulf Stream that separates the Bahama Banks from the Florida peninsula. In the sixteenth century, the Bahama Islands as they are now known were all referred to as the Biminis, whereas now the Bimini Archipelago refers only to the chain of small islands a short sail across the Gulf Stream east of the Florida peninsula. Today, the legend of the Ponce de Leon search for the Fountain of Youth has variously been interpreted as a search for 'riches', or merely a search for clean potable water. South Bimini Island the largest of the diminutive chain of islands possesses about a dozen freshwater wells and may well have served as a 'watering' waypoint for Ponce and later Spanish mariners.

After sailing up the Gulf Stream, or perhaps through the Bahama Islands Ponce eventually made his way west across the Gulf Stream to the Florida peninsula. It is unknown exactly where Ponce landed. It may have been around Cape Canaveral or the Melbourne Beach area, or further north, where legend has it he discovered a safe harbor and a well with clean water at an Indian village named Seloy, the eventual site of present St. Augustine. Later, in 1521 Ponce returned to Florida and sailed through the Florida Keys into the present Gulf of Mexico, then along the southwest Florida Gulf coast. On both the

Atlantic and Gulf coasts of Florida Ponce met with hostile natives, first the Ais tribe on the Atlantic coast, and then the Calusa on the lower gulf coast. On his Gulf coast voyage, Ponce was wounded in a skirmish with the Calusa and later succumbed in Havana from complications of his wounds.

The next incursion into the Gulf of Mexico was the disastrous Panfilo de Narvaez expedition of 1528. Narvaez, sailing from Havana landed at present Tampa Bay and dispatched a contingent of troops under the command of Cabeza de Vaca (his name translated literally as "Head of the Cow") on an overland route along the Florida Gulf Coast. Narvaez was to rendezvous with the de Vaca party along the northwest Florida coast but failed to show up. De Vaca and his party had no choice but to push on to the west, where after a decade of hardship a few stragglers made it to a Spanish Mission in present-day New Mexico. The Narvaez expedition was followed by the Hernando De Soto expedition of 1539. De Soto fared somewhat better, and made a long rambling expedition through the American southeast, wresting provisions from the native populations, and infecting them with deadly European diseases, notably smallpox. Eventually, the De Soto expedition reached the Mississippi River where De Soto died, and as the story goes his corpse was placed in a hollow log weighted down with rocks and interred in the Mississippi River.

Formation of the Platoro Group

When Paul Znika returned to Gary, Indiana he met with his brother Max and other would-be treasure hunters, where he told of his adventures on Padre Island, his meeting with Billy Kenon, and what he believed to be the potential for treasure hunting in the waters off of Padre Island. It took Paul and Max about a year to marshal their forces in Indiana and form a company that they eventually named "The Platoro Group". The name Platoro is a contraction of two Spanish words, "Plate" (silver) and "Oro" (gold) that combined as Platoro spelled only one thing — treasure! The Znika brothers conducted additional research in university libraries, and through further conversations with Billy Kenon, became convinced that the coins recovered on

Max Znika in white shirt waves at the camera while aboard Little Lady.
Standing next to him is Clyde Means.
Photo: Billy Kenon

the beach near the entrance to the Port Mansfield channel came from the Spanish shipwrecks that were lost in 1554.

A memo by the first Platoro Group attorney, John Stiles chronicles the early days of the shipwreck project. Stiles writes that in the spring of 1965 Paul Znika organized an expedition to Padre Island that was equipped with a magnetometer and a search boat. This initial foray into the field found nothing. Later in the summer of 1965, Paul Znika launched another survey that found nothing. Participating in this search were Paul and Max Znika with others that will reappear in this book named Steve Gersack, Ray S. Tittle, Sr., and Ray S. Tittle Jr., Orville Tittle and Clyde Means. In the spring and early summer of 1967, Paul Znika organized another group consisting of the above-named individuals along with Joe Emsing and attorney Stiles. At this point, the Znika brothers formed Platoro Limited Inc. an Indiana Corporation. Another group was mentioned in the Stiles memorandum, named the California Group, and later another group named the Camden Group (NJ) became involved. These two groups of 'would be' treasure hunters will appear later in this book.

After these two forays into the field that failed the Znika brothers contracted with Billy Kenon who had a workboat named the *Little Lady*; Billy would soon become the head of the field operations off of Padre Island, and the others named above fell into a secondary role in various capacities as the Platoro Group began operations under Kenon's direction. To be sure there were growing pains within Platoro, but over time Kenon and the *Little Lady* and a few trusted divers assumed command.

One important question was asked early on by savvy investors as the company was being formed: were there any Texas laws that would preclude the Platoro Group from searching for shipwrecks offshore of Padre Island, and then if they found evidence of such a wreck site would they be able to salvage the shipwreck? The answer was not a clear-cut yes or no! There is a body of law, Admiralty Law that pertains to marine salvage, and the right of an individual or corporation to search for, locate a shipwreck and then salvage that abandoned wreck. There were also state laws and regulations that addressed submerged resources like mineral rights in state waters along with a myriad of fisheries and environmental issues. However, there was no specific legislation that addressed sunken historic shipwrecks, or nothing that lawyers saw as an obvious impediment to the treasure hunt.

However, at the time, there was some treasure salvage history that was being written on the Atlantic coast of Florida, along a strip of shoreline that would come to be known as the 'Florida Treasure Coast'. As the Platoro Group carried out research and began to organize in Indiana to search for Spanish galleons in the Gulf of Mexico, a treasure hunter in Florida had made an earlier discovery that had ushered in a long and troubled relationship with State of Florida officials, which should have given the Platoro Group cause for concern, if not outright worry.

Some background to this earlier Florida discovery is in order. In the late 1950s, Kip Wagner, a retired building contractor who had settled near Sebastian Inlet on Florida's east coast, discovered the re-

In an attempt to dredge up coins from the beach on Padre Island, Billy and his crew strung a net on a 40-foot frame, which they dragged along the seafloor from shore. They found nothing but "sand dollars". Photo: Billy Kenon

mains of a shipwreck in the shallows south of Sebastian Inlet some forty miles south of Cape Canaveral. Wagner and some associates formed a group that they named the Real Eight Corporation, after the Spanish Eight Reale coins, (Pieces of Eight) that had been discovered over the years on beaches along the Florida east coast. Eventually, the remains of eight Spanish shipwrecks would be found lying in the shallows between Sebastian Inlet and the vicinity of Fort Pierce Inlet, a distance of about thirty-five miles. These shipwrecks would prove to be the wreckage of a Spanish fleet, the victims of a storm in July of 1715.

As at Padre Island, the first indication in Florida that there was a nearby treasure ship was the presence of coins on the beach that had been found by Wagner and other beachcombers using surplus, World War II, and later, more user-friendly commercial metal detectors. Eventually, Wagner decided to get wet and utilizing a surfboard with a plexiglass viewing window ventured into the shallows near a Wagner weekend retreat on the beach strand, several miles south of Sebastian Inlet. As the story goes the ocean was calm, almost like glass, and the sun was high in the sky. Wagner wore bathing trunks and was equipped with swim fins, a dive mask, and snorkel for breathing.

As Wagner paddled out into the ocean he saw the white sand bottom with areas of crushed seashells. About thirty-five yards out he observed a raised limestone reef, then more sand until about seventy-five yards from shore he saw a raised pile of round rock that marked a ballast pile, then two anchors and a half dozen cannon encrusted with camouflaging sea life. At this point, Wagner knew that he had found a shipwreck site and that the coins found on the beach had likely come from this shipwreck.

After the discovery of the shipwreck site, Wagner and his group contacted the State of Florida, who at that time had no specific agency that dealt with shipwreck resources. They did have an agency named the Internal Improvement Trust Fund that administered leases on state lands. The law in Florida stipulated that the governor and his cabinet, as owners of all the submerged lands under the state's navigable waters, had oversight of any entity that sought the use of these bottomlands for any purpose. Wagner applied for a salvage lease that covered a fifty-mile area from Sebastian Inlet south to a point near Stuart, Florida. Looking back at the Wagner, Real Eight experience in Florida, there was nothing in the Florida law and regulations that would have given Platoro an early warning that legal storms were on the horizon. As a matter of fact, the Florida salvage program could have easily been adopted by Texas.

The State of Florida's arrangement with Real Eight would be amiable at first, but as the salvage operations grew, and more shipwreck sites were discovered the state seemed to lose control as treasure hunting morphed from a cottage industry to a business. When Mel Fisher joined with Real Eight as a sub-contractor the salvage operations continued to expand, as Fisher began to find significant amounts of treasure. Fisher had an intensity and desire to be the "World's

Greatest Treasure Hunter" that set him apart from the Real Eight Corporation, a group that took a gentleman's club approach to treasure salvage. Quickly, the relations between the State of Florida and the treasure hunters began to deteriorate, and the authorities in the capitol at Tallahassee began to tighten their controls. The state hired Carl Clausen, an underwater archaeologist to supervise the treasure hunters in the field, and then hired agents and placed them aboard working salvage vessels to record and document the treasure discoveries, and prevent the pilfering and theft of treasure. At this point, the treasure salvage industry turned into two distinct camps, treasure hunters, and their state regulators.

The first few years of the Real Eight salvage operation in Florida proved that there were millions of dollars in gold and silver at the bottom of the sea and that the new "Aqua Lung", the self-contained underwater breathing apparatus (SCUBA) technology made it possible for just about anyone with the money and inclination to join in the search for riches underwater. After the discovery of treasure off the coast of Florida, the flood-gates opened. Mel Fisher soon became the most successful treasure hunter working in Florida and elevated a part-time avocation to a full-time profession. Fisher would eventually make his mark as the treasure hunter who discovered the riches of the 1622 Spanish shipwrecks, the *Atocha* and *Santa Margarita*, in the Marquesas Keys some thirty miles southwest of Key West.

In Texas, Platoro might have had the foresight to see 'the writing on the wall'! Texas had a long tradition of local, as well as state-wide pride in Texas history. The Alamo Historic site in San Antonio was a favorite cultural destination, as was the San Jacinto Battlefield, near present Houston, where Sam Houston and a small army of Texans, defeated a larger Mexican army led by General Santa Anna, and in small part avenged the killing of Jim Bowie, Davey Crockett and the other defenders of the Alamo garrison. Billy Kenon and the Znika brothers understood the pride that Texans took in their heritage; in hindsight perhaps it was naive for the Platoro Group to believe that Spanish treasure galleons, bound from Mexico to Cuba, would not be considered part of Texas patrimony or, as a Texas State official would later allege, belonged to the "Schoolchildren of Texas".

The Spanish Conquest of Mexico

The early exploration of the New World was not carried out under any unified strategy. In the aftermath of the Columbus Era, the Spanish Crown along with Governors in Hispaniola, Puerto Rico, and Cuba launched expeditions through the Bahamas into the Atlantic as well as into the Gulf of Mexico. The islands of the Caribbean had yielded little gold and the indigenous native populations of the islands were wiped out within a generation. The goal of the early Spanish expeditions was simple and direct. They intended to discover and acquire the purported wealth to be found in the New World and search for a semi-mythical El Dorado, a "City of Gold". In 1513 Balboa made the arduous crossing of the Isthmus of Panama to the Pacific Ocean. Soon the Spanish made their way down the Pacific Coast of South America where they discovered the fabled 'Mountain of Silver' at Potosi in present-day Bolivia.

Almost from the beginning of the Padre Island treasure hunt the principal members of the Platoro Group, the Znika brothers and Billy Kenon understood the origin of the coins on the beach, and firmly believed that a treasure ship lay somewhere offshore near Port Mansfield Inlet. Academics and government officials generally believe that treasure hunters have no interest in history, nor in the archaeology of the ships that they salvage. This is not true! From the beginning of the Padre Island expedition, Billy Kenon knew that the coins were part of a larger consignment of precious metals (gold and silver coins and bullion) that had originated in Mexico and had been shipped on a Spanish treasure ship, from the port of Vera Cruz. Billy also knew that there were yearly shipments of treasure from Mexico and South America, and each year Spanish treasure fleets carried a year's-worth of treasure to the port of Havana where the combined riches of the America's were then shipped on to Spain. The coins that had been found on the beach at Padre Island had come from one or more of these vessels, and the Platoro Group believed that if they did not investigate the origins of the coins, which is the provenience of the treasure, then the history of the shipwrecks would never be fully known.

After the voyages of Ponce de Leon along the east and west coast of Florida and the incursion of Hernando De Soto into the

Florida peninsula, the Spanish soon realized that Florida was going to be devoid of gold, much like the islands of the Caribbean. However, the Spanish were not about to give up their quest for riches. In 1517 the Governor of Cuba, Diego Velazquez de Cuellar, dispatched his brother, Hernando Cortez on an expedition into the Yucatan peninsula of Mexico; on this expedition, Cortez heard tales of riches to be had to the north in what is now Central Mexico. In 1518 Cortez departed on another expedition this time with eleven ships manned by 100 sailors and 500 soldiers. The powers that be in Havana had tried to block the departure of Cortez, and the conquistador, in what amounted to a mutiny, departed against the Governor's orders.

Cortez landed on the gulf coast of Mexico and established a settlement named La Villa Rica de Vera Cruz, close to where the present port city of Vera Cruz is situated. Again, Cortez encountered natives who advised him that there were riches inland and offered to lead Cortez to the source of this wealth. Whether the natives were attempting to aid Cortez or just get rid of the Spaniard by sending him onward with promises of riches, is difficult to tell. As in North America, there were native tribes of various strengths and the Indians would join in various allegiances, and routinely war amongst themselves. The Spaniards with their steel-edged weapons, muskets, and cannon made particularly attractive allies for native chiefdoms.

Cortez began to plan his invasion of central Mexico in the face of some opposition by elements of his own expedition. As the story goes Cortez scuttled ten ships of his fleet at Vera Cruz, executed some potential mutineers, and retained one ship as a dispatch vessel to be used later. Soon, with some Indian allies, Cortez began to move inland. After a series of pitched battles against Aztec warriors, Cortez approached the City of Teotihuacan, now present-day Mexico City on November 8, 1519. In a terrible tactical blunder, the Aztec Emperor Montezuma attempted to befriend and placate Cortez. With his sizable army on the right battlefield, Montezuma could have crushed Cortez, regardless of the Spaniard's horses, artillery, armor, firearms, and native allies.

When Cortez realized the extent of the gold and silver resources that Montezuma controlled the conquistador undertook a daring kidnapping of the Aztec Emperor on 14 November 1519. Soon after abducting Montezuma the ruthless Cortez had Montezuma strangled, and in a series of daring tactical battles fought his way out of the native capital, all the while, consorting with local tribes to regroup and conquer the Aztecs. Through this strategy of divide and conquer Cortez was eventually able to subdue the Aztec Empire. Upon word of what Cortez had accomplished and the riches of the territory that was to be named 'New Spain', Cortez returned to Cuba and was hailed as a hero.

Soon colonists began to flock to the port of Vera Cruz, and present-day Mexico City was built on the ruins of the Aztec capital of Teotihuacan. In short order the Spanish discovered the Aztec silver mines at Taxla. Eventually the combined gold and silver resources of Mexico would come to rival those of Peru. In 1524 the Council of the Indies was established to administer the treasure resources of Mexico (New Spain) and South America (Terra Firme). The King of Spain appointed Viceroys (Royal Administrators) to administer the colonies and to supervise the mining and refining of precious metals into coin and bullion of required weight and purity. The Viceroys were also tasked with supervising the transport of the gold and silver coins, bullion and crafted jewelry carried on the treasure fleets that made the yearly return voyage to Spain. In time the members of the Platoro Group would understand the full story of how a Spanish treasure would come to rest in the shallows off of Padre Island.

Into the Field at Padre Island

In early 1966 the Platoro Group had raised enough money to begin field operations. The Znika brothers had kept in close touch with Billy Kenon, and common sense dictated that Kenon, an experienced waterman, would head the field operations since he owned a vessel that fitted the operation's needs, the 50-foot *Little Lady* a converted U.S. Navy landing craft, the perfect salvage vessel for working in shallow coastal waters.

Since the coins discovered on the Padre Island beaches had largely been discovered along a three-mile expanse of shoreline north of Port Mansfield Channel, it made sense to begin search operations in this area. The Znika brothers reached out to several remote sensing experts and corporations that might aid in their search efforts. The Znika contacts were Cal Miller from Michigan who was brought on board in 1963 and then a year later in 1964 Bill Strooby and Jack Haskins began to conduct remote-sensing surveys off Padre Island as well. Strooby and Haskins, with ties to the State of New Jersey, were referred to as the Camden Group.

Much to Billy's frustration over four years (1963-1966) the alleged 'experts' found nothing. The Znika brothers also contacted another remote sensing guru, Harold 'Doc' Edgerton who suggested, because so many coins were found on the beach near the inlet, that the group perform a remote sensing magnetometer survey around the mouth of the inlet. The General Dynamics Corporation considered utilizing one of their pioneer miniature submarines in the search, the forerunner of modern remotely operated vehicles (ROV technology). Unfortunately, the waters off Padre Island were found to be too shallow for the deployment of the submarine, however, an important magnetometer survey began in August 1967. Earlier that year Billy, on a diving expedition, discovered an unidentified iron object and a silver coin on the bottom about two miles north of the inlet.

Remote sensing is the bread and butter technology of modern treasure hunting, and the proton magnetometer was the tool of choice. A magnetometer is an instrument that registers the presence of iron objects lying on the seafloor or buried in bottom sediment. Platoro began to tow the magnetometer "tow fish" on a cable behind a small survey boat while the onboard operator-technician watched the console for the tell-tale spikes on graph paper. Spikes registered on graph paper indicated the presence of ferrous material lying or buried in bottom sediment. These might be iron objects like anchors, cannons, and ship fittings that indicate the presence of a shipwreck site. In the vernacular of treasure hunting and remote sensing technology, unidentified objects are referred to as anomalies. As the magnetometer survey was being conducted, and as various passes were made along the shoreline the "mag" began to record the presence of iron material on the seafloor. As the mag recorded an anomaly, the magnetometer operator shouted, "Hit!", and a crew member would toss a buoy on a weighted line over the side to mark the location of the anomaly.

Billy initiated a magnetometer survey in the wake of the above-mentioned failures, and after a couple of weeks Billy noticed that the buoys were clustered in two areas, the first about two miles north of the Port Mansfield channel entrance, along with a second anomaly cluster an additional mile farther to the north. As the buoys were thrown to mark the anomaly positions, divers from an accompanying chase boat went over the side in an attempt to ascertain if there was any shipwreck material exposed on the bottom. At first, all the divers observed was sand and shell; this indicated that the iron objects were buried and would have to be excavated.

Here the Platoro crew is seen launching a specially constructed, non-magnetic pontoon float for deployment of a Varian magnetometer.
Photo: Billy Kenon

Billy Kenon made many of these diver-verification investigations. Billy noted that the water was about twenty feet deep, almost always murky, with visibility only about three feet, except for a few days during the 'doldrums' of the summer when visibility became markedly improved. This lack of visibility and the fact that no shipwreck material, like anchors or cannons, was visible on the bottom meant that Platoro would have to adapt, or design, their own sediment displacement system in order to remove the overburden that covered a possible historic shipwreck.

About this time the Znika brothers contacted Mendel L. Peterson at the Smithsonian Institution in Washington D.C. and advised Peterson that Platoro was searching for what was believed to be a Spanish shipwreck off the coast of Padre Island. The Znikas asked Peterson if he would serve as an archaeological advisor to Platoro, and Peterson consented. After Billy Kenon and his fellow divers began to find shipwreck artifacts and treasure, and the Platoro Group was forced into an adversarial relationship with the State of Texas. Some of the criticisms levied against Platoro were that they did not retain an underwater archaeologist, did not make a shipwreck site plan, nor did they keep accurate field notes and records. These allegations were clearly not true. From the beginning of shipwreck excavations, Billy Kenon and his dive team had taken direction from Peterson and kept daily worksheets, and as the excavation went on they developed an archaeological site plan that marked the position of all the artifact material and treasure that was discovered.

Mendel Peterson was a former naval officer who had served with distinction in World War II. In the navy Peterson had become a qualified deep-sea diver and after his discharge had pursued a graduate degree in history from Vanderbilt University in Nashville, Tennessee. In the post-war period Peterson became the curator of Naval History at the Smithsonian Institution in Washington D.C. While at the Smithsonian, Peterson conducted the archaeological salvage of the *H.M.S. Looe*, a colonial period British man-o-war that had been lost in the Florida Keys in 1744. Peterson also carried out underwater excavations in Bermuda

Right: Mendel Peterson, Naval Historian at the Smithsonian in Washington D.C.

with Teddy Tucker, the Crown appointed 'Receiver of Wreck' and along with Tucker was considered a pioneer in underwater archaeology. Peterson became extremely interested in the mystery of the 1554 coins recovered on the beach, and when he began to receive the magnetometer data that recorded two discrete anomaly clusters north of Port Mansfield Channel, he began to conduct serious research in the archives. It did not take Peterson long to suggest to Platoro what they already suspected was the origin of the coins — the Spanish Plate fleet of 1554.

Generally, academics and cultural professionals hold treasure hunters in low esteem. It is certainly true that shipwreck sites have been looted and valuable archaeological information has been lost, never to be recovered. On the other hand, many treasure hunters like the Platoro Group act responsibly and hire professionals like Mendel Peterson as consultants and closely follow the directions that these experts provide. In the early 1960s, underwater archaeology was in its infancy; there were only a few academic and professional archaeologists that had the expertise to consult in underwater archaeology, and state governments had virtually no ability to aid or supervise underwater excavations.

Navigation and Bad Weather

As the Platoro Group conducted their remote sensing survey off of Padre Island, Mendel Peterson began to gather information on the treasure fleets that sailed from Mexico in the period after the defeat of the Aztec Empire. First, in the immediate aftermath of the Aztec subjugation, there were lone voyages, or small fleets of vessels that sailed to Havana, and then Spain, with the riches that had been wrested from the Aztecs. The Aztec treasure consisted of gold and silver objects that the natives had made and had been used as ornamentation or jewelry. Often these objects in the form of native religious objects were considered idolatrous, and the Spanish melted them down into portable bullion.

Later in 1535 a mint was established in Mexico City and coins were struck, and bullion bars were cast and then shipped on to Spain.

Due to the danger of lone vessels carrying treasure being intercepted by rival nations and pirates, Spain began to implement the "flota" or fleet system that offered protection against piracy, but no protection against the elements. Each year, generally in the spring two great shipments of treasure originated in the New World. The New Spain (Nuevo Espana) fleet originated in Mexico at the port of Vera Cruz, and the South American, or the Terra Firme fleet originated on the Pacific Coast of present Peru at Callao. Smaller fleets like the four vessels of the New Spain 1554 fleet were the exception rather than the rule.

On April 9th, 1554 four Spanish vessels the *San Esteban*, the *Espiritu Santo* the *Santa Maria de Yciar*, and the *San Andreas* departed Vera Cruz on a trans-gulf voyage to Havana. The vessels were transporting New Spain's contribution to the yearly treasure fleet that would later sail in a combined convoy from Havana to Spain. The three vessels that would eventually be lost off Padre Island sailed out into the Gulf of Mexico into what is known as the "Loop Current", a clockwise flowing current that flows along the north littoral of the Gulf of Mexico then empties into the Straits of Florida. It is impossible to know what the weather conditions were in the gulf when the small fleet departed Vera Cruz. It is safe to say that the four vessels would have attempted to sail as far out in the gulf as possible, well out of the sight of land, before picking up the current that would carry them to Havana.

The shipwreck of the three Spanish vessels was believed to have occurred on or around April 29th 1554. The vessels were lost either in a storm, through navigation error, or a combination of both. The archives (Ojos 1554) contain only a notation that cites the tragedy simply stated, "Her loss was due to bad weather that took it to the coast of la Florida." Another archival note (Quesada, 1554) blames "the lack of caution by pilots and sailors" for vessel loss. There were survivors of the shipwrecks and their memoirs were included in the Ojos and Quesada archive.

Two of the Spanish archival annotations bear close scrutiny. First, the information that the small fleet departed on April 9, and did not wreck off Padre Island until April 29, 1554, gives the student of maritime history and navigation immediate concern. The twenty-day voyage from Vera Cruz to shipwreck off Padre Island had taken an inordinate amount of time; in twenty days the three ships should have been well out of the Gulf of Mexico and approaching the island of Cuba, and the port of Havana. Also, the archival notation that shipwreck took place off La Florida is puzzling; the three vessels when lost were nowhere near Florida, or the Florida coast. What went wrong with the little Spanish fleet?

It is very likely that after departing Vera Cruz the ships did not sail far enough out into the gulf in their attempt to catch the Loop Current and prevailing winds that would have eventually carried them into the Caribbean and on to Cuba. It is also probable that until they

were caught in the bad weather they were affected by either varying winds, or crosswinds, that kept them close to the coast, not out in the open gulf where they could, with some luck and expert seamanship, ride out a storm. Blaming the pilots and sailors may be translated as the simple fact that the navigation technology at the time could not warn the ship's masters that they were too close to shore, or nowhere near the coast of La Florida.

One of the issues in working out a wrecking theory is the question about the speed of the vessels or in other words, trying to determine how far and how fast the vessels had sailed before they were lost. The vessels of the time measured speed across the water by throwing a block of wood attached to a line overboard and then measuring the time it took for the ship to pass that block. Generally, with a good wind, aided by the loop current, a sailing vessel could make about three to four knots per hour. A ship's master would sail with lookouts aloft during both day and night; in bad weather, they would increase the watch to ensure that any sighting of the coast would call for a turn seaward. The coast of Mexico as well as what is now the coast of North America was generally low relief, there were few if any elevated landmarks, and in a haze that was caused by dust-storms or lightning-ignited brush fires, the shoreline could be obscured, and with ensuing poor visibility, a vessel could run aground or run ashore. The gulf contains some rock formations that qualify as patch reef, however, the danger in the Gulf of Mexico is shoaling water that can occur some miles offshore.

Reconstructing a voyage from short archival entries is difficult. Contemporary coastal cruising directions for yachts under sail warn mariners to avoid the doldrums of the Big Bend region of the Mexico–Texas coastline where winds are erratic and there is a weak coastal current. The four Spanish vessels would have been carried along by a combination of southeastern prevailing winds, usually stronger in April, combined with a northward-flowing surface current. These forces would have carried the small fleet to a point off the South Texas coast where the clockwise rotating Loop Current would have pushed the fleet into the arc of the loop and on to Havana. According to the Quesada archive, it took them nearly three weeks (twenty days) to travel from Vera Cruz to the point near present Port Mansfield where the three vessels were shipwrecked. Avoiding the Big Bend region of the present Mexico-Texas border a direct dead-reckoning voyage from Vera Cruz to the present Port Mansfield area is about 750 kilometers or 460 miles.

The three Spanish vessels were lost in mid-April well before the hurricane season. It is most likely that the ships encountered a severe cyclonic thunderstorm that generated accompanying inshore waves, exacerbated by shallow water. Caught in this system and unable to make way against the power of the wind and ride the storm out in deeper water, the three vessels began to founder and soon ran aground in the shallows off Padre Island. During the Platoro salvage operations, an anchor was found seaward of the *Santa Maria de Yciar* that possibly indicates that the crew could see that they were being driven ashore, and attempted to arrest their shoreward drift. In any case, the three ship's final resting place was in the nearshore shallows off a low relief barrier island, the nature of which was known only to the hostile natives that the Spanish castaways would meet in the days that followed.

Deep Digging

In the first two weeks of August 1967, a remote sensing survey of a two-mile swath of the shallows off of Padre Island was conducted by Billy Kenon and the Platoro crew. At night the magnetometer team camped on the beach at Padre Island to ensure that they could get an early start at first light. The data from the survey showed a concentrated cluster of anomalies at a location several miles north of the entrance to the Port Mansfield ship channel and this location was selected as the initial target to be examined.

The first phase of diver verification in about twenty feet of water showed no trace of shipwreck or associated shipwreck artifacts. Billy, along with the other Platoro divers began to attack the buried anomalies with a standard airlift. An airlift is an apparatus that generally consists of a six-inch diameter tube that has an accompanying source of pressurized air that is directed into the airlift from a deck-mounted compressor. The effect of air expanding in the tube creates a vacuum and lift whereby bottom sediments are drawn upward through the tube and deposited nearby where the sediment can be checked for small light artifact material. Often the airlift expels sediment into a nearby small boat or barge where the sediment is further screened and examined.

Billy and the excavation crew found that excavating with the airlift apparatus made for slow going, and soon it became apparent that the suspected shipwreck remains were buried at some depth in sediment that called for a more powerful and intrusive excavation technology. For example, in a day of digging, the divers could only penetrate about six feet of sand, then they began to encounter a few bits of debris, a few historic period ship's fittings, along with some modern fishing and shrimping debris from coastal trade, as well as a retrospective of trash such as soda bottles and beer cans.

At the end of a day of excavation the *Little Lady* would return to base camp that had been established at the north side of the Port Mansfield jetties; the next day they would return to the site and find that the excavation had been completely filled with drifted sand. There were a number of reasons for this dynamic coastal environment that included nearshore current and moderate tidal changes, some occasionally heavy wave action associated with storms, along with silting from nearby Port Mansfield Channel. Billy and his cohorts began to discuss how they were going to excavate to a depth where possible shipwreck artifacts might possibly be found.

Throughout the 1960s a large number of coins had been found near the entrance to the Port Mansfield ship channel, and a colonial period anchor had been recovered during dredging operations; locals had come to call this site "Money Beach". This would later lead to the possibility that one of the shipwrecks had been destroyed when the channel had originally been dredged in the mid-1950s. The ship channel had originally been constructed to allow large commercial vessels the opportunity to access Laguna Madre and the Texas mainland that lay behind Padre Island. Once the channel was dredged, two extensions of reinforced concrete jetties were placed on either side of the cut; these were intended to stabilize the channel and impede the silting that takes place in natural inlets, as well as artificial inlets.

It was soon apparent that constant dredging by the U.S. Army Corps of Engineers would be necessary to keep the channel open and navigable. Within a mere five years after construction, the concrete block jetties began to settle, disappearing into the soft sand of the Gulf of Mexico. Once the jetties disappeared beneath the surface the channel began to silt-up, and an ebb shoal was created at the entrance to the channel. An ebb shoal is a large sub-surface sandbar, that when situated at the mouth of a channel or inlet, often makes navigation impossible. Once the ebb shoal formed, only small shallow-draft vessels like Billy Kenon's, *Little Lady* were able to navigate the channel.

The bottom line with respect to the Port Mansfield Ship Channel was that after millions of dollars of construction the sad truth was that the dream of bringing large, deep-draft shipping into Laguna Madre was never realized. Port Mansfield Channel was both a blessing as well as an impediment to the salvage project. In a positive sense the channel allowed quick and easy access to the Gulf of Mexico for Platoro work vessels. The downside was that twice daily through tidal action the channel discharged thick silt out into the gulf that was carried up-shore and down-shore in the current. To say the least, the channel was a mixed blessing.

One of the Platoro Group members was from California and brought a small prop-wash system from the west coast to the Texas Gulf coast. For various reasons, vessel size, and flaws in the construction of the system, only about six feet of sand could be excavated, which was not deep enough to reach the anomaly material recorded during the magnetometer survey, and not much deeper than the diver operated airlift system could dig. Nevertheless, Billy Kenon was impressed with the basic design of the mechanism and began to fabricate an improved excavation system of his own. This deflector utilized a similar prop-wash sand displacement system but was very different than the aluminum dog-leg shaped prop-wash deflector that had been utilized with outstanding results by Mel Fisher on Florida's Treasure Coast.

A few years into the 1715 shipwreck excavations the same problem of moving deep drifted sand began to plague the Kip Wagner Real Eight operation. In the 1960s Mel Fisher had revolutionized treasure hunting with his development of the mailbox, prop-wash system. When Fisher arrived on the Florida Treasure Coast in 1965 he brought a contraption that he called the prop-wash deflector, nicknamed the "mailbox". Some background is in order.

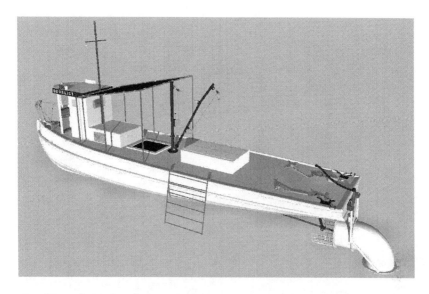

Kip Wagner's Real Eight Corp. adapted their vessel, the Derelict, to function with a 'mailbox', or prop-wash as seen here. The Derelict operated in Florida while Billy Kenon's Little Lady performed similar excavations in Texas. Illustration: T. L. Armstrong

The mailbox got its name from its dog-leg shape that indeed resembled a post office mailbox. Constructed out of sturdy aluminum and light steel, the mailbox was affixed to the stern of a salvage vessel in an upright, or lift position. When the salvage vessel reached a site to be excavated the vessel would be secured in place with three anchors, a bow anchor, and two stern anchors. The anchors were transported to their respective positions utilizing a small outboard motorboat, then dropped overboard and set in the seafloor.

Once the salvage vessel was anchored in digging position the mailbox was lowered by hand using a crank, or hydraulically lowered in place, with the mouth of the mailbox facing the double or single props. In this position, the long, tube section of the prop-wash apparatus pointed directly down to the seafloor. The tricky and potentially dangerous aspect of securing the system in the digging position was having a diver drop over the side of the salvage vessel into choppy water and fix several pins that secured the mailbox to the hull of the vessel. In choppy water, a diver could lose fingers or mangle a hand if the pins were not worked into place swiftly and deftly. A prop-wash

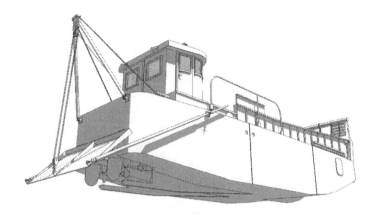

The Little Lady was modified to drive her prop-wash downward on an angle using a deflector, rather than using the tubular 'mailbox' design favored by Florida salvors. Illustrations: T. L. Armstrong

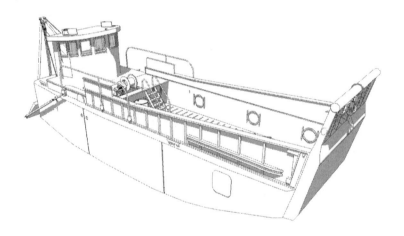

system operated properly could dig a deep hole or trench, but could also carefully dust-off a site, allowing divers to work around the system when it was operating. Sometimes experienced divers could work beneath a salvage vessel when the prop-wash was engaged and were able to retrieve artifacts as they became exposed in the sand.

Based on the proven potential of prop-wash systems in Florida, Billy Kenon began to work on his own design for a deep-digging excavator. Instead of the common prop-wash configuration, Billy designed

The Little Lady is seen here with her deflector engaged dockside.
Photo: Billy Kenon

a reinforced plywood and steel deflector that was square-shaped rather than round. This modified deflector could be lowered into position beneath the prop of the *Little Lady* and served as a conduit for prop-directed water to be forced down toward the sea-floor. Unlike the Mel Fisher system that directed water downward to dig a circular crater that quickly began to fill in, Billy's mechanism slowly excavated a 20 foot wide by 40-foot long trench that could be gradually widened and lengthened.

When Billy activated his system he found that he could dig deeper and faster than other team members could while using any of the other dredge-systems. To test the excavation capacity using his newly designed system Billy selected a close to shore anomaly that proved to be the lower hull of a turn-of-the-century sailing vessel. It took about a day to fully expose the ship's hull, and the test was valuable as a training exercise; strangely the hull was devoid of any artifact material that could closely date the wreckage. Later in his salvage career, Billy began using a seventy-five-foot vessel named the *Rio Bravo*, equipped with twin prop-wash deflectors. The *Rio Bravo* was one of the largest and most powerful salvage boats utilizing prop-wash deflectors that had ever worked on Florida's Treasure Coast. In seventy feet of water, the *Rio Bravo* could excavate sediment to a depth of twenty feet.

On the second day that Billy used his new dredge system, he dug down about fifteen feet and encountered the shaft and ring of a large colonial period ship's anchor. Immediately there was euphoria among the Platoro Group. It appeared that the magnetometer survey had indeed located what might be an historic shipwreck. Once Billy had his prop-wash deflector working properly, the team began to remove large amounts of drifted sand overburden.

Seen here at the stern of the Little Lady from left to right are Kirk Purvis, Billy Kenon, two unidentified men, and George Purvis.
Photo: Billy Kenon

From the beginning of the project, word had spread that the Platoro Group was onto something at Padre Island. The Znika brothers had a tough time saying 'no' to individuals that they thought could

Billy Kennon holds a plank recovered by Kirk Purvis standing to his left. The plank was found beneath the ballast pile of the Espiritu Santo, circa 1967. Photo: Billy Kenon

help the project, either by providing equipment or personnel. During the period when the remote sensing survey was underway several groups approached the Znika brothers and offered aid. The most visible were the two groups referred to earlier, the California Group and the Camden, N.J. group. Although both groups hung around for three years, the relationship between the two groups and Platoro was more informal than formal. Daily worksheets for individuals from both groups have survived, including those of Fritz Karr, Richard Pasqual, Kirk Purvis, Tom Rose, Tim Seltenrich, and Bill Strooby. Billy Kenon recalls that he counted on Kirk Purvis and Tom Rose during the excavation phase of the project and to varying degrees on the others during the remote sensing and also during the all-important excavation phase of the project. Billy remembers the experienced treasure hunters, Jack

Haskins and John Potter as being marginally in the picture along with Jeff Burke, a Texan, who had been the Mayor of a small town named Rio Hondo. Burke owned a crop duster aircraft that was designed to fly low and slow and was perfect for reconnaissance flights along the coast. While Billy and his team were magging and diving, Burke and Haskins were occupied flying the shoreline, looking for signs of a shipwreck from the air. As time went on Billy Kenon and Jeff Burke began to clash; Billy thought that Burke was a "grandstander" who refused to stick to plans and schedules and insisted on taking auxiliary boats and divers on wild goose chases up and down the coast checking out rumors and false leads.

Treasure, Archaeology, and Hurricane Warnings

On September 13, 1967, the *Little Lady* had excavated to a point where the large anchor was almost completely exposed and artifacts began to appear. That day a large silver plate was found near the anchor along with a valuable navigation instrument called an astrolabe. Over the course of the season, three astrolabes were recovered on the site; only one was fully complete and still operable. As the artifacts were recovered they were marked on a site plan that the divers utilized to measure their progress and record their finds. Soon they began to recover large clumps of coins and a nearly complete crossbow. Excitement began to spread, and the Znika brothers found it difficult not to talk to the press and otherwise spread the news that the Plataro Group had found a major shipwreck site. Billy's feeling was that the euphoria that accompanied the discovery of coins and artifacts was natural and ultimately good; however, Billy constantly worried that 'loose talk' and publicity would bring unwanted attention to the project and create an aura of jealousy that could ultimately cause problems. Billy recalls that there was also none of the hooting and shouting and the exchange of high fives as often captured in contemporary television documentaries of treasure hunts. Billy believed that among the core group of divers there was a pervasive no-nonsense approach to the project that made the team cohesive and successful.

Billy Kenon and the Platero Group, like the Kip Wagner, Real

Eight Corporation in Florida were, in a sense, working in a void as far as performing archaeology underwater was concerned. The decade of the 1960s had ushered in a new specialty in archaeology, to wit: underwater archaeology. The more famous pioneer practitioners of this archaeological specialization were two Americans, Peter Throckmorton and George Bass, as well as the Platoro archaeological advisor, Mendel Peterson. Peter Throckmorton had learned his discipline in the Mediterranean where, as an accomplished SCUBA diver, he had observed hard-hat Greek sponge divers harvesting sponges that grew on the ancient shipwrecks that lay on the seafloor. The sponge divers prized the large sponges that grew prolifically on the ancient nutrient-rich shipwrecks that had over the centuries become artificial reefs. Unaware of the cultural value of these wreck sites, the divers with their heavy steel-toed boots would work their way across the shipwrecks harvesting the sponges while at the same time destroying the fragile amphora and wooden superstructure of these vessels, many of which dated to the Bronze Age.

George Bass was an academic who specialized in classical archaeology; Throckmorton was a journalist, expert photographer, and gifted field archaeologist. Throckmorton approached Bass, who was not yet a diver and showed Bass photographs that documented the destruction of the shipwrecks. Throckmorton explained to Bass that if there was not a program of rescue archaeology and associated sponge diver awareness, that in another decade these non-renewable shipwreck resources would be lost for all time. Throckmorton believed that the sponge divers could be educated about the damage that was being done and that the sponge divers could also lead archaeologists to other valuable shipwreck sites.

Bass was hooked and a new sub-discipline of archaeology was born. Throckmorton taught Bass to dive and together the two returned to the Mediterranean where they led a series of University of Pennsylvania expeditions that excavated important Greek and Roman shipwrecks. The earliest Throckmorton–Bass expedition was to Cape Gelidonya in 1960, where the Penn team excavated a Bronze Age shipwreck at just about the same time that Gus Znika was driving down the beach on Padre Island in search of his own shipwreck.

With the work of Throckmorton and Bass in the Mediterranean, the new sub-discipline of underwater archaeology was born. It was the contention of the two underwater pioneers that they were not doing "underwater archaeology"; they were doing "archaeology underwater". In other words, the same rigor used by archaeologists on land excavations had to be performed in the infinitely more technically difficult realm of undersea excavation.

At the Smithsonian, Mendel Peterson was aware of the rigor that was required in underwater archaeology. Peterson was writing a book titled *History Under the Sea* that dealt with site excavation, artifact interpretation, and artifact conversation. Peterson believed that Billy Kenon and the excavation team, with some expert tutoring, would be able to follow the basic requirements of scientific archaeology that required setting up a datum point on a baseline that bisected a shipwreck site, and then implementing a grid system over the site. Within each grid, artifacts would be carefully excavated and their position marked on the master site plan so that later an interpretation could be made of the shipwreck. Peterson's book also stressed the importance of recording and recovering any remaining hull material, especially remains of the ship's keel that often was preserved in drifted sand.

The Platoro divers returned each day to the site where a previous grid had been cleared and a new grid awaited excavation. A centerline had been placed down the middle of the site in a northwest-southeast direction that would prove to divide the largely intact ships ballast pile in half. The three ships anchors that lay on the site were excavated and their locations were recorded at the northwest extension of the site. As artifacts were encountered their position in a particular grid were marked and they were then tagged and removed to the deck of the *Little Lady*. Once on deck, the tagged artifacts were placed in wet storage, and the divers either returned to the artifact trail or fired up the deflector and excavated a little deeper. The dive team did not move ahead until a grid was entirely clear of artifacts; if there was more overburden in a particular area the deflector was activated and the sand dusted away. This process was continued until bedrock was reached, an indication that a particular area was clear of all artifact material. One of the most difficult physical efforts was the removal of ballast to ascertain if cultural material had worked down into the cracks and fissures between the ballast. Often it was slow going, but gradually the site was covered by the dive team.

Billy relates that as the dive team worked their way across the site that there was a sense of urgency and none of the ego-driven behavior that he was to see later on in his salvage career. As a diver located an artifact or a concreted fused-together clump of artifacts, the grid position was noted on an underwater slate. A diver would then return with the artifact to the surface and hand it off to a deckhand who placed the artifact in wet-storage. Billy relates that during the artifact recovery that egos were checked at the door It was not that Billy Kenon or Kirk Purvis found an astrolabe or a clump of coins, it was the team that got the credit for a discovery, and that find ultimately became a Platoro team discovery. Billy recalls, that as the artifacts were recovered they entered the chain of custody that ultimately carried the artifacts to Gary, Indiana. Billy also believes that without the newspaper publicity that goes with most treasure hunting projects there was no distraction to contend with, only business as usual — finding more treasure!

Billy and the team knew that the preliminary remote sensing survey had indicated that there was another possible shipwreck site just a mile to the north. Some of the extended Platoro team who were not particularly good divers, having time on their hands, wanted to break away from the excavation and investigate this site. The Znika brothers at Billy's urging vetoed the two site excavation plan and with the support of Mendel Peterson insisted that all the efforts would be invested on the site that was producing spectacular artifact material each day. As it turned out the site to the north that Platoro recorded during the remote sensing survey was later excavated by the State of Texas with some modest success. This site has been tentatively identified as the remains of the *San Esteban* and will be discussed at some length later in this book.

Mendel Peterson, the Platoro archaeologist, was a historic firearms and munitions expert and was particularly excited about the discovery of crossbows that had been buried on the site for over three hundred years. Fortunately, many of the artifacts had been quickly buried in the oxygen-free sediments that had settled over the shipwreck were in remarkably good condition. As Peterson came to learn, the crossbows were crafted from a particularly fine example of spring steel, with a cat-gut bow-string that was used to power the "bolt", the short iron and wood crossbow arrow, or quarrel, as arrows were often called in the colonial period. Peterson had been working on a book about historic weapons and intended to include the crossbow information in this new publication. According to Peterson, the crossbows were particularly interesting and important because they were not the standard Spanish military-type bows but smaller more streamlined weapons that were used primarily for hunting. Peterson offered a tentative reason for the presence of the hunting bow on the shipwreck as opposed to the heavier military style bow. Peterson believed that the military-style bows were heavier and more robust because they were primarily utilized against European forces who wore armored breastplates to protect their vulnerable vital organs. Peterson's theory was that the natives of the new world, not having iron armor, or the long gun, the harquebus, of the Spanish, could be successfully repulsed or killed using the smaller lighter hunting crossbow.

In a project report that was produced from the daily log sheets the Platoro attorney, John Stiles, summed up the artifact recoveries on the shipwreck site that would later be tentatively identified as the

There were a number of smaller crossbows found on the Espiritu Santo wreck as remodeled here, unstrung. The reference ruler is twelve inches in length.
Illustration: T. L. Armstrong

Espiritu Santo. Stiles writes, "Without attempting to set out the entire inventory, it should be indicated that they consisted of hundreds of 16th-century Mexican coins, three extremely rare marine astrolabes, various sizes of cannon and cannonballs, crossbows, ships fittings, silver bullion, a gold ingot, and a small gold cross."

Photographs of the artifacts were immediately taken and sent to Mendel Peterson at the Smithsonian. Peterson was excited by all of the finds, but of all the artifacts recovered he found the astrolabes to be the most impressive. Peterson requested that any marks or inscriptions on the astrolabes be recorded so that their makers, place of origin and date of manufacture could be researched later. Peterson had also given the divers and support staff a crash course in artifact conservation. Iron objects were placed in freshwater to stabilize them before undergoing the 'electrolytic conversion' where the accumulated salt

*One of several astrolabes recovered by the Platoro group on the
Espiritu Santo. Photo: Billy Kenon*

A small gold cross recovered by the Platoro group on the Esperitu Santo.
Photo: Billy Kenon

that led to rust and deterioration would be 'leached' out of the artifacts. Coins and other iron objects like ships fittings underwent the same process. The team had excavated a number of the previously cited crossbows that were a combination of iron and wood; the wood underwent a process where the salts were flushed out of the wood, and a polymer was then used to preserve the wood. The larger the iron artifacts were, like cannon and anchors, the longer that they had to spend in the electrolytic reversal process, a process that could take a year or more.

There had been a conversation about whether to keep the artifacts in Texas, and stabilize them there, or transfer the assemblage elsewhere. Following the advice of Mendel Peterson, the Znika brothers established an artifact holding facility ashore where the artifacts were held for a short time in wet storage, stabilized, photographed and recorded on artifact sheets, then the material was transferred to Gary, Indiana. In Gary, the brothers owned a space that had once housed their "Dairy-Quality-Check" ice cream factory where they further processed, conserved, and stored the artifacts, utilizing burial vaults that were adapted to conservation and artifact holding tanks.

The main reason the artifacts were transferred to Gary, Indiana was at the request of Mendel Peterson. Peterson was based in Washington D.C. and intended to closely monitor the artifact preservation process with periodic trips to the Indiana conservation facility. Peterson contended that a straight flight from Washington D.C. to

Gary, Indiana was quicker and more cost-effective than a convoluted trip from Washington D.C. to Port Isabel, Texas, that was 'off the beaten track' of airline routes. Shipping the artifacts out of state was a management decision that would eventually cause Platoro some trouble as would internal conflicts that had been brewing for some time.

The euphoria of the finds was contagious! Billy found that the extended group of divers, boat operators and project hangers-on seemed to come together and cooperate as a group. They could all smell the success that came with hard work, luck, and the comradeship that the excavation of the shipwreck site was bringing. However, Billy noticed that one of the group seemed to be unexcited about the finds, and even negative, as the artifacts were recovered from the bottom and brought on board the *Little Lady*. This was Jeff Burke, the crop-duster-mayor from Rio Hondo. In the euphoria generated by the finds, Billy did not see the internal storm on the horizon, but a real storm of epic dimensions was about to hit the Texas coast. That same afternoon, on September 19th, 1967, the group heard the first weather forecasts that a hurricane, named Beulah, was headed toward the Texas coast and the Padre Island salvage site.

The Platero Group had spent approximately a month in the field before the arrival of Hurricane Beulah in 1967. Beulah struck the Texas coast early on the morning of September 20th, 1967 south of Port Isabel, in the border town of Brownsville, with winds measured at 140 miles per hour. The storm rapidly moved inland across south Texas on the 21st, wreaking wind damage and flooding from the intense rain. Billy Kenon and the Platoro salvage team rode out the storm in Port Mansfield, and outside of the 'downtime' caused by the wind and rain, Platoro came through the storm relatively unscathed. Hurricane Beulah, rather than a slow-moving storm that pushes a storm surge ahead, was a rapidly moving, wind and rain event. Following the storm Billy took the *Little Lady* out to Padre Island and noted that the face of the beach had changed very little; the remains of a campfire that the group had left on the beach prior to the storm had not been affected at all, no storm surge washed the beach clean, only the heavy rains filled Laguna Madre on the leeward side of Padre Island, and flooded the low lying coastline. Billy made the first dive in the area where the buoy had been left attached to the shaft of a small boat anchor. Of course, the buoy was gone, but the anchor and the remains of the rope were in their original position.

Early on in the Padre Island shipwreck investigation, Billy and his associates made a walking survey of the beach dunes opposite the shipwreck site, only about a hundred yards beyond the low tide line. This stretch of beach and dunes was the area where the survivors huddled in the aftermath of the shipwreck. Billy and the other investigators believed that there had to be some remnant of the salvage camp; perhaps, the survivors had buried some treasure in the dunes? At the time of the shipwrecks, the Gulf of Mexico east of Vera Cruz was devoid of any European habitation, there were no settlements, missions, or Spanish forts anywhere along the gulf coast, all the way to Florida.

The Marooned of 1554

Most, if not all near-shore shipwrecks have associated salvage camps, or camps where survivors gathered after being shipwrecked. This was true with the Florida 1715 shipwrecks as well as the Padre Island shipwrecks. These camps were utilized as a refuge to recover from the trauma of their shipwreck ordeal, and then to serve as a temporary safe haven to await rescue, or launch a foray to reach a nearby settlement or port. Probably the best-known survivor and salvage camp is associated with the Spanish 1715 shipwrecks in Florida. In the aftermath of the 1715 shipwrecks, the survivors could see the battered remains of their vessels stranded in the near-shore shallows and the wreckage strewn shoreline. Almost immediately the castaways would have started to comb the shoreline recovering items that they needed for their immediate survival as they awaited possible rescue. The 1715 wrecks that were salvaged in the modern era by Kip Wagner, and Real Eight, and Mel Fisher's Treasure Salvors, were near-shore sites strung out for some thirty-five miles between Sebastian Inlet and the vicinity of Fort Pierce Inlet on Florida's south-central east coast.

With both the 1715 shipwrecks in Florida and the 1554 Padre Island shipwrecks, the storm left the grounded vessels in various stages of destruction. Most were dis-masted; some had lost their sterncastles and upper decks. This wreckage floated ashore and with wave action and storm surge, and may have eventually come to rest on the beach well above the high tide line. Contemporary beachcombers talk about finding coins that have washed ashore. This was true with the Padre Island wrecks as well. "Washing ashore" has several connotations; one implies that they were lost offshore in shipwrecks gradually making their way along the bottom moved by current, tide and wave action. In reality, coins and artifacts found on the beach found their way to shore in the clothing of drowned sailors and ship's passengers, and on the buoyant wreckage that washed ashore. For example, a sterncastle is where many of the treasure chests were stowed and where the ship's officers and elite wealthy passengers berthed during the voyage. When the sterncastles and upper decks broke loose in a storm, this shipwreck material would wash ashore, and in the dynamics of wind and wave, valuable goods and treasure became strewn across the near-shore shallows and the beach itself. Even during the storm much of this treasure was buried and not discovered until centuries later when the beach-dunes were cut-away by winter storms and hurricanes.

Both the 1715 and 1554 shipwrecks had hulls loaded with silver and other treasure; however, lying in the shallows they could not be salvaged until rescue vessels arrived with proper equipment and specialized personnel. The survivors, after establishing camps with lean-two shelters, and kindling fires to dry their clothing, began to search the beaches for treasure and other valuables. It is easy to picture the scene after one of the shipwrecks, the shoreline is scattered and strewn with human bodies and wreckage. Many of the corpses carried personal wealth and contraband, many had purses with coins, other bodies were found to have gold chains wrapped around their torsos, hidden by their clothing. In the Spanish Colonial period, the gold chains and the links that made up the chains served as a currency, somewhat comparable to an individual gold or silver coin. The person with the chain who wished to make a purchase would merely snap off one of the links from the chain and make a purchase with the link. Some of the sailors who were a desperately poor element of society would have been scavenging the shoreline for treasure, clothing and other valuables. Small groups of crew and survivors established their own camps, and in the hours of darkness, individual coins, small gold bars, and other items of treasure, like jewelry, were lost. There was also gambling, fighting, and even robbery and murder as lawless elements roamed the shoreline.

As Spanish officers regained control of the shipwreck sites order was restored along the beach. Almost immediately the survivors suffered from exposure to the elements, the hot sun, and hard-driving afternoon rainstorms. Florida is only habitable today because of the advances of mosquito control services provided by the government. In the eighteenth century, the marshes that lay west of the barrier islands were teeming with mosquitos that feed on human blood. According to Spanish chronicles, shipwreck survivors were tormented to the point that they would bury their children up to their necks in the sand to alleviate in some small measure the tormenting bites of swarms of mosquitos. Another remedy was to live within the smoke of campfires that kept the mosquitos at bay. Unfortunately, the 1554 castaways had more than voracious mosquitos to contend with.

The Espiritu Santo Salvage Continues

After the hurricane, Billy and the Platoro divers immediately returned to work. As stated previously, the buoys that marked the site had been disturbed, but the fast-moving, rain dominated storm, did nothing to disturb the shipwreck site lying on the bottom of the Gulf of Mexico. The divers continued to move through the shipwreck site utilizing Billy's unique prop-wash deflector to move overburden, followed by the use of an airlift to excavate down into the ballast pile, The rotating teams of divers logged in the artifacts, and marked the finds on the site plan grid by grid. Once the site was largely cleared of artifact material the site plan began to reveal information that Billy and the crew could utilize to make an analysis of the site itself; including how the vessel had wrecked, or in nautical terms, "came to grief" in the Padre Island shallows.

First, it was necessary to try to figure out the attitude of the ship, in other words in what azimuth was the wreckage lying in the near-shore shallows. They also needed an answer to this question: where was the bow and where was the stern of the vessel? The ballast pile was somewhat scattered, an indication that over time the hull had deteriorated as it was buffeted by wave action and worked by the current. Also, much of the hull might well have been removed by later salvage efforts where grappling hooks might have been utilized to pull the vessel apart. Often ship's hulls that were intact and with deck planking remaining were set afire and burned to the waterline in order to expose the cargo holds. And there was also the work of ship-worms that would slowly eat-away a ship's exposed hull.

Taking the entire shipwreck site into consideration along with consultation with Mendel Peterson it was theorized that the ballast pile lay in a north-west to south-east configuration, with the bow of the vessel to the NW and the stern to the SE. Ballast was scattered on both the port and starboard sides of the wreck site, with the starboard to the NE, and the port side of the vessel to the SW, aligned generally with the shoreline. It was fairly easy to ascertain the stern of the vessel. This was where the majority of the silver coins were discovered along with the majority of the silver discs that were likely carried in the stern-castle area of the ship. Balancing the treasure cargo lying at the stern of the vessel, were three ship's anchors that were stowed near the bow of the vessel; one broken anchor lay amongst the scattered ballast on the starboard side of the vessel roughly amidships. The scatter of the cannons on the site also bears scrutiny. The large Lombard cannons were found in place on the site lying in the ballast pile in roughly the same position where they would have been stowed on the vessel at the time of the shipwreck. The guns, although scattered, were generally aligned along the port and starboard sides of the ship, where they would have been brought into action during a battle at sea. Three small breech-lock swivel guns were discovered generally clustered together on the port side of the vessel. These rail guns would have been carried stowed, especially in rough weather. Swivel guns are usually small and relatively light in weight, two to three feet in length, although some large swivel guns may measure five feet in length. These guns can be handled by one man; when a ship is going into action, a swivel, or rail gun, will be picked up and dropped into a slot in the rail and thus brought into action as an anti-personnel weapon, shooting small shot at enemy sailors who are within close range, as in attempting a boarding action. Four swivel guns were marked on the site plan and salvaged along with

A number of bomardettas, or 'Lombard' cannons were found on the Esperitu Santo by the Platoro group, along with verso swivel guns. Illustration: T. L. Armstrong

fifteen larger, Lombard cannon. Five of the large Lombard guns were found scattered on the starboard side of the vessel amongst scattered ballast; it's unknown if these guns were lost during the wrecking incident or later at the time of the first salvage in 1554–1555. It is interesting that these large and valuable artillery pieces were abandoned on the site and not retrieved later as other salvage boats plundered what remained of the shipwrecks.

The treasure on the *Espiritu Santo* turned out to be a bit of a disappointment to the young salvage crew. At the time of the modern salvage in the 1960s Billy and his cohorts were not aware of the extensive salvage that had been done by the Spaniards, and in the years thereafter by many other looters. A gold bar was found in the middle of the ballast pile, and is referred to as a finger bar because of its small size and long narrow shape; this was an indication that perhaps a number of gold bars were salvaged from this location and that this lone bar was overlooked, or lost in the salvage process. There were only two gold bars recovered during the entire salvage, one during Platoro's work on the *Espiritu Santo* wreck, and later by the State of Texas investigators on the northernmost wreck, the *San Esteban*. Both bars had ends that were clipped indicative that the two bars had been checked for purity.

The silver bullion that was recovered from the surmised stern area of the *Espiritu Santo* was in the form of discs, often called "splashes" because of their shape. Although the gold was shipped in rough ingot form, the disc form of silver bullion was a forerunner to silver bullion in large 90-100-pound silver bars. The term "splash" refers to their varied irregular shapes. The splash ingots were made by bringing the silver to a molten form and then pouring the silver into small, shallow, impressions dug in the ground where it quickly hardened. The individual splash ingots were then collected, dusted off and packed for shipment on the treasure vessels.

As the site was being excavated Billy and the salvage divers began to make plans for moving up-shore to the northernmost site, the *San Esteban*, and then perhaps taking on the deep drifted sand of the 'ebb shoal' in front of the Port Mansfield Ship Channel. Having completed the *Espiritu Santo* excavation the crew of the *Little Lady* was eager to continue the salvage. The Znika brothers were pleased with the progress the Platoro team had made, as was the project archaeologist, Mendel Peterson.

'Busted'
The State of Texas Intervenes

It's sad to say, but many treasure hunting operations meltdown through internal squabbles and feuds. The term "treasure fever" describes what happens psychologically to some treasure hunters when the desire for wealth overcomes good sense and judgment. Very few people get rich, or even make a living, from treasure hunting. The high costs of field operations, the money or artifacts that have to be distributed to investors, and the difficulty marketing artifacts often make it hard to turn a profit. The more partners or associates that are involved in a project, the more the profit must be divided. By nature, treasure hunters are obsessed with secrecy and rely on non-disclosure agreements when dealing with outsiders, fearful that interlopers will 'pirate' a site, or locate an associated shipwreck site that may have been transporting a richer cargo. Often paranoia takes over, and there are, to be sure, cases of claim jumping, pilfering or more extensive theft, and on occasion — murder.

Treasure hunting and marine salvage, like any specialized business, requires that there be a division of labor where individuals are trusted to perform specific specialized functions. There was no doubt that the Znika brothers were the project managers at Padre Island and had to answer to investors and other outside interests. Billy Kenon, because of his background in marine salvage, and local ties and knowledge was the obvious choice for the supervision of the project in the field. Billy personally liked both Znika brothers, but also maintains that from the beginning of the operation, "that there was no unified leadership" — rather it was 'government by committee'. Billy maintains that the brothers had been successful in their Indiana business, but treasure salvage is not corporate America and calls for a certain style of charismatic leadership, where the boss must be both forceful, and at the same time accommodating; the bottom line is this: the leader can't be a nice guy.

If the discovery of treasure was a catalyst for internal dissension, there were early warning signs that an internal storm was on the horizon. Treasure hunting can be boring; navigating what seems to be endless magnetometer survey lines in a hot, cramped boat, and excavating in hard, compacted seafloor sediment is not fun like finding artifacts and treasure. A research design and field plan must be prepared and closely followed. From the beginning of the magnetometer survey and continuing through the excavation phase of the project, some of the team exhibited impatience to the point that if nothing was recorded on the magnetometer or artifact recoveries were infrequent, they wanted to break off operations and move to another area, and begin searching anew. Even after the divers began to find treasure, right after Hurricane Beulah, it was often difficult to keep some divers searching in a particular area, following a path where an artifact had been found, until another artifact was discovered. Billy believed that if the search was thorough, foot by foot across the site, all of the artifact material would eventually be found. Conversely, if the search was haphazard, and the team jumped around from one area to another then artifact material and treasure would certainly be missed, and it would be impossible to return to a previous position or spot. Everyone felt good about the *Espiritu Santo* site and were looking forward to the prospect of excavating the two remaining wrecks.

Generally, when a treasure hunting operation is shut down, it happens on the high seas with a Coast Guard or State Marine Patrol boat approaching, perhaps with sirens blasting, and armed officials on deck who board the treasure hunter and confiscate the artifacts on the spot. This was not the situation on December 13, 1967, after the *Little Lady* and the salvage crew had spent a productive day on the shipwreck site. The Platoro Group had been working the site since September 12, 1967, and over some ninety days had recovered hundreds of artifacts that were placed in wet storage and taken ashore to a warehouse to be processed. Most of these artifacts had already been transported to Gary, Indiana where further stabilization and conservation were being carried out under the guidelines established by Mendel Peterson.

On December 13, 1967, as Billy remembers, the *Little Lady* returned to the dock at Port Mansfield around noon after a hard morning of offshore excavation. As they were tying up they were approached by two Texas Rangers who identified themselves, and in a low key manner advised Kenon and the crew that the State of Texas, in the guise of The General Land Office, had obtained a temporary restraining order against Platoro, and from the serving of the order they were barred from any further salvage in Texas waters. Reading the small print Kenon learned that the judge who signed the order was Paul Martineau of the Twenty-Eighth Judicial District located in Brownsville, Texas. As Platoro would come to learn the rationale used to shut down the salvage was soon to be tested in court. As the State of Florida had argued, the state owned the bottomlands and mineral rights in state waters and that meant that they owned the treasure that lay on the seafloor off Padre Island as well.

The official responsible for the takeover of the Platoro site was an elected politician named Jerry Sadler, the Commissioner of the General Land Office. Sadler knew that the treasure and artifacts had been removed from the site, and he moved quickly to affect their return. Later in a monograph describing the Padre Island artifacts and treasure, Doris Olds from the Texas Historical Commission wrote,

"Texas citizens had raised the question of ownership of the Spanish Galleon Treasure since it had been recovered from state tidelands." As it turned out Olds would be another apologist for Texas authorities, and Sadler in particular. It was Sadler who spearheaded the attack on Platoro that would be litigated not only in state and federal courts but also in the court of public opinion.

Shortly after the State of Texas shut Platoro down, John Stiles the group's attorney prepared an affidavit timeline that formalized his opinion on what had precipitated the shutdown of the Plataro operation. Stiles writes, "The state was talked into taking such action by a local individual who had been an informal member of the group and had been allowed to tag along. After the find, he thought he should be one of the directors of the operation, and had been asked to leave." There was also an allegation that the shutdown of the salvage project was precipitated by newspaper articles describing the treasure and artifact discoveries. Billy Kenon states that this is untrue; over the period that the site was being salvaged, Billy says that there were no newspaper articles or television reports that the wrecks had been discovered, or were being excavated. Kenon says that it was internal friction caused by a disaffected team member who went to the Texas authorities and blew the whistle on the shipwreck excavation.

Billy Kenon confirmed the 'whistleblower' as the crop duster pilot and Mayor of Rio Hondo, Jeff Burke. As Attorney Stiles had written, Burke had tagged along and treated the hunt for the shipwreck as a great adventure; he was one of the individuals who hated to stick to a research plan and was often away, playing the big shot, searching for shipwrecks from the air with Jack Haskins, John Potter, and the other adventurers who spent more time hanging around than working. Later, in a 1981 "Valley Morning Star" newspaper article the press went directly to the Znika brothers for a read on Burke; the Znika brothers maintained that "Burke was not a member of the (Platoro) corporation." Burke maintained that he had met the Znika brothers on the beach at Padre Island where they were prospecting on the beach around the entrance to Port Mansfield Channel.

John Stiles, in a thumbnail history of the Platoro Group, had written about his due diligence in researching salvage law in Texas at the time Kenon began field operations. Stiles writes, "Prior to engaging in the salvage operations, the law of Texas had been researched by counsel (Stiles). It was determined that Texas had no law dealing with the licensing of such marine archaeological operations, as had been the case in the State of Florida. At the time Plataro began operations in the field, Florida was the only state in the union that had legislation dealing with the issue of treasure salvage."

Everyone associated with the Padre Island shipwrecks knew that there would be a long, hard fight to recoup treasure and recover any expenses that Plataro had incurred during the salvage effort of the *Espiritu Santo* shipwreck. Texas officials lost no time traveling to Gary, Indiana where the treasure was confiscated, or in legal terms, 'arrested'. The history of the Padre Island treasure after the court order was invoked has been documented by Doris Olds at the Texas Archaeological Research Laboratory of the Texas Memorial Museum. Olds sums up the situation just after the court injunction was served; Olds writes, "The Plataro Group had retained an attorney and had filed suit almost immediately after the court order seizing the treasure was invoked at sea, on the docks at Port Mansfield, and later in Gary, Indiana. In simple terms, the treasure had been placed into the safekeeping of the State of Texas pending a future court's decision concerning the ownership of the collection — this was the office of Jerry Sadler in Austin."

Walking Home to Mexico
The 1554 Castaways Death March

Archival accounts of historic shipwrecks are often valuable, but sometimes constitute a labyrinth of second and third-hand information and even dis-information. However, there are exceptions; the dispatches of Pedro Menendez de Aviles, the first Spanish Governor of Florida are remarkably straightforward and accurate. Menendez was a field commander, he understood what he had observed, and wrote accordingly. This is contrasted by the memoirs and stories written by some Spanish clerics that cross the line from a historic account, to an account where the truth has been 'corrupted' in an attempt to preach or make a religious statement. As discussed earlier, the 1554 shipwreck victims on Padre Island would have found themselves in the same predicament as the 1715 shipwreck survivors one hundred and seventy years later. According to a Spanish chronicle (Davila), the 1554 survivors gathered together on the shoreline, and soon after, began to march south along the coast to a destination that lay ahead, a settlement named Panuco, near the Rio Panuco south of the present Rio Grande then known as the Rio Bravo.

It seems that the 1554 castaways had no idea of exactly where they were, or how far it was by land to Vera Cruz. The archivist Davila wrote that they did not carry any substantial foodstuffs with them, nor did they attempt to salvage or construct a small boat that they might have sent for help. Was there a lack of leadership among the survivors? An experienced mariner or military commander would have immediately begun to salvage valuable items from the stranded ships, then they would have constructed a small camp or fortification. Cannons would have been available as would have been ships timbers to cobble together a redoubt or breastwork for protection against hostile natives. There would have been ample foodstuffs on the stranded vessels and the soldiers had harquebuses (the long rifles of the era), crossbows, swords and other edged weapons that could be utilized for offense and defense.

The decision by the Spanish shipwreck survivors to set out south along the beach in an attempt to reach Mexico was undoubtedly based on the belief that Vera Cruz was only a three or four-day hike away, south along the beach. This is difficult to understand since the small fleet had been at sea for some twenty days before they were wrecked at Padre Island. It may have been that the trauma of the shipwreck had effected the reasoning of the castaways, or their leader.

The ability of the castaways to walk to Vera Cruz was based on two unknown variables, the distance back to Mexico, and the potential danger posed by the Indians that lived along the coast. The castaways would soon encounter untamed and untested tribal people who had, without doubt, experienced Spanish slave catchers and other hostile Europeans. The Indians that encountered the 1715 shipwreck victims in Florida were only a shadow of the fierce natives that had greeted the first Spanish voyages to Florida in the early sixteenth century. All of the early Spanish conquistadors had encountered the Indians from a position of strength. Early accounts, like those of Ponce de Leon, report that the Spanish were initially repulsed by hostile natives; however, even powerful Chiefdoms like the Calusa on the southwest coast of Florida were eventually conquered by the overwhelming Spanish force of arms. When Pedro Menendez de Aviles encountered the Calusa in 1566 he found them to be fierce and unaccommodating. Mcnendez and his landing party became engaged in a pitched battle with tribesman on Mound Key near present-day Fort Myers. Menendez was a formidable figure; the Calusa soon came to understand that Spanish force-of-arms would prevail in any further hostile encounters. Menendez formalized his relations with the Calusa by taking the daughter of Chief Carlos as a symbolic wife.

The tribe that lived on the mainland east of Padre Island was named the Coahuiltecan (Co-wal-te-can). Not much is known about these people, and they did not leave a particularly rich archaeological record. Europeans, however, were not entirely unknown to these natives; the survivors of the ill-fated Cabeza de Vaca and Tristan de Luna expeditions had passed through this territory some five years later in 1559. It should be noted that de Luna passed through this territory unscathed; whether through luck or for some other unknown reason the de Luna party survived an epic trek across nearly the entire lower littoral of North America.

The Coahuiltecan Indians lived primarily on the mainland, but paddled to the barrier islands to hunt, fish, and gather bird eggs. No doubt, from the time of the shipwrecks, the castaways had been under surveillance by natives hiding in the dunes. The tribesman would have been particularly interested in the shipwreck booty that lay in the shallows, and as the survivors regrouped onshore the natives counted the available Spanish survivors, should they attack or wait until the survivors weakened, or departed, strung out along the Padre Island shoreline? From the time that the shipwreck survivors made it to shore, they would have made easy targets for Indian arrows and war clubs.

One narrative of the 1554 shipwreck castaways is recorded in a memoir by Fray Agustin Davila Padilla. The 1554 shipwreck historian Robert Weddle, in *The Nautical Archaeology of Padre Island*, describes the Davila narrative as a homiletic narrative or account of the castaway's adventures. The word "homiletic" is a term that refers to a preachy account that reads like a tedious sermon' This account by Padilla was written some years after the fact, and as Weddle pointed out, the Spanish sometimes had a propensity to write fanciful memoirs and histories, full of religious bric-a-brac and calling on the Holy Virgin for mercy and intervention in their trials and tribulations!

Sometimes an account of a historic incident is written well after the fact and suffers in the re-telling. Padilla was born forty years after the shipwrecks occurred, and his written account of the plight of the shipwreck survivors was cobbled together from various sources. One such source was Father Vicente Paletino de Corzula, a Dominican priest who wrote, "In the year 1554, some ships were coming from New Spain which wrecked on the coast of Florida at the Rio de Las Palmas. There all the Spanish were killed with arrows. Among those who died were five friars of the order of St. Dominic. The Indians left thinking everyone was dead; but one friar Marcos de Mena, covered with wounds, arose, traveled at night, by day he stayed in the earth. In this manner, he traveled to Panuco, and he recovered his health."

The Davila archive reads like an adventure story. The survivors from the three shipwrecks gathered on the beach and together under the command of the Captain-General of the 1544 fleet, Andres Lopez de Archuleta, set out south toward habitation in Mexico. The party made headway at the speed of the slowest walker, which must have been the women, children, and aged members of the party. The most pressing danger that faced the castaways as they marched south was the debilitating effect of the sun and the lack of potable water. Rain on Padre Island is intermittent, and the little water that exists is found in small brackish pools in the interior of the island.

After a reported seven days on the trek, a party of about one hundred Indians approached the bedraggled party of Spaniards. The natives were armed with bows and arrows and had brought an offering of food, primarily of fish for the Spanish to eat. Fires were lit and the women prepared the fish while the Spanish kept their weapons ready for a possible attack, if, in fact, the Indians' act of friendship was a ruse. The détente between the Indians and the Spanish continued while the Europeans ate, then suddenly the Indians loosed a volley of arrows at the Spaniards. The Spanish were armed with crossbows, examples of which were recovered from the wreck of the *Espiritu Santo*. The

Spaniards were also armed with swords, pikes, and knives. In the short battle that ensued three Indians were reportedly killed; there were no Spanish casualties.

After this first encounter, the Spanish party continued along the shoreline, interspersed with patches of marsh and shallow wash-overs and inlets. In the second week of the march, the weaker Spaniards began to fall behind and were individually killed, picked off by the Indians. The Spanish column had thus far been protected by cross-bowman who served as skirmishers and as rear guard. After marching a few more days the depleted party crossed an intertidal area where a free-flowing river emptied into the Gulf of Mexico. The Spanish knew this river as the Rio Bravo, and have kept this name till today; in America it is known as the Rio Grande.

At the Rio Bravo, several rafts were fashioned from driftwood bound together with cordage that had been carried on the trek. While crossing the river the crossbows that had been bound together, fell into the muddy river and were lost. Having crossed the river the party continued south. Soon the Indians returned and at a distance continued to harass the party with volleys of arrows. When the Indians realized that the Spanish no longer had their crossbows, they began to close in and engage the Spanish in individual combat. The Spanish swords were no match for bows and arrows shot from close quarters, and soon the Spanish casualties began to mount. The Spanish noted that the Indians, after killing their compatriots, would mutilate their bodies, and preoccupied with this endeavor seemed to lose interest in the immediate combat at hand. Not all of the Spanish that were taken by the Indians were killed; several were captured and merely stripped of their clothing. When the Spanish observed this, they began to strip themselves, believing that if they relinquished their clothing they would be spared immediate execution.

South of the Rio Bravo, the terrain changed appreciably; instead of sandy beach, there were long stretches of bay-fringed-marsh interspersed with mangroves that made the journey more difficult and rugged. Further on there was another river named the Rio de Las Palmas, the River of Palms, which flowed down from mountains, through jungle lowlands before emptying into a bay with surrounding lagoons and marsh-lined tidal wetlands.

The Davila account of the castaway's plight then falls into a more prurient account of shame brought on by the Indians stripping the castaways of their clothing and the final assaults of the Indians on the decimated band of Spaniards. As the strung-out fugitives struggled towards the Rio Palmas the women and children had gone ahead, in part to hide the shame of their nudity from the male members of the party. According to the chronicles, as the women and children drank from the River of Palms they were attacked again by the Indians, and being unable to defend themselves they were quickly massacred. Davila wrote, "As they lay gasping for breath between gulps of water, the Indians attacked again. It was a pitiful sight: naked women and children trying to pull arrows from their bodies; screaming children running to helpless mothers for protection; mothers slain while pausing to help a child; or seeing their children wounded, unable to help without being killed themselves. It was at this time that a stalwart and inspirational member of the party, Dona Catalina de Ribera was killed."

In some sources that describe the return march to Mexico, the argument is made that the castaways were harried by the same tribe of Indians over the course of their entire march to civilization; this is highly unlikely. The historian Robert Weddle writes, "It, therefore, seems improbable that any one band would have pursued the travelers outside its territory; not all the tribal groups were friendly with each other." The Spaniards must have passed from the land of the various Coahuiltecan bands living north of the Rio Grande into that of other diverse groups south of the river and eventually between Las Palmas and the Rio Panuco, into the country of the Huasteca (Was-teca) tribe.

Davila wrote that after the massacre of the woman that some two hundred men were left. Special attention is given to the party of friars that felt a special shame being stripped naked in front of the women, children and their male peers. The special plight of the Catholic priests was a recurring theme in all of the narratives that stress the martyrdom of the clergy and is one of the continuing themes in Catholic homiletics. Davila records the last moments of one of the priests named Fray Diego, writing, "Fray Diego weak from his wounds and lack of nourishment, fell into the sand and announced, 'I can go no farther, Trust to God, Brother Hernando, and commend me to his Divine Majesty'. Davila continues in his own words the end of Fray

Diego, "God took Fray Diego to eternal life after the purgatory of this experience (which was God's will)". The account ends with Fray Hernando digging a grave in the sandy river bank where he buries his dead companion.

The account of the castaway's march reads in part like a serial adaptation of a much-embellished story. Over the entire march, the Spaniards are constantly sniped at by the Indians. After the Europeans lose their crossbows in the Rio Grande they are at the mercy of the Indians. The Spanish soldiers armed with swords, pikes, and daggers can keep the Indians at bay, but the Indian tactics would then become obvious. Instead of closing with the Spanish all they needed to do was approach within the range of their bows and arrows and let loose a volley. The arrows were likely tipped with stingray barbs and would only have been fatal if they struck a vital organ. The archivists tell of Spaniards with three or four arrows protruding from extremities attempting to pull out the arrows but eventually succumbing to infection and the infestation of maggots in their wounds. No doubt stragglers would have been hunted down; then killed with knives fashioned from shell tools, or the Spaniards own edged weapons. Torture was also inevitable, and death for many of the Spaniards would have been slow and agonizing.

The men that reached the Rio de Las Palmas found the slaughtered woman and children, and then made their crossing. Some found a canoe and while crossing the river encountered some small whales (more likely Porpoise) that capsized their canoe. Swimming to a small island they constructed a raft out of driftwood and branches that they used to float to the south bank of the river. This party then found other dead compatriots that had made an earlier crossing.

The next river that the Spanish reached has been identified as the Tanipa. Here a small party of Spanish were about to cross the river when they saw several canoes full of Indians paddling down-river toward the gulf. Hiding in the tall grass at the river's edge, the Spanish were attacked by stinging ants. To relieve the agony of the stings they retreated into the river and were spied by the Indians, then killed as they attempted to swim to safety.

One of the most astounding stories of any of the Padre Island shipwreck castaways was that of Fray Marcos who had allegedly been shot with seven arrows as he attempted to cross the river. (This is reminiscent of the Catholic St. Sebastian martyrdom story) None of the wounds were immediately fatal, but the priest was unable to walk. Fearing he was going to die anyway his companions buried him in the warm sand with only his face exposed; then they departed. Sometime later the priest recovered his senses, in part, it was stated, from the restorative warmth of the sand. Digging himself out of the sand the padre continued on south down the coast for four days to the next river, the Rio Panuco.

The priest lay on the north bank of the Rio Panuco, unable to cross. Eventually, he was spotted by a band of unarmed Indians who wrapped him in a blanket, laid him in a canoe and paddled to the south bank of the river. There they bathed and fed the priest, tended to his wounds, and when he felt stronger they continued south to a Spanish settlement near present-day Tampico, the Spanish Mission of Tamaholipa.

The exact time frame of the shipwreck victim's ordeal at Padre Island is inexact at best. One chronicler computes the tragedy from time of shipwreck until the lone survivor reached Tampico to be 42 days. The common belief of historians of the period is that the Spanish knew of the shipwrecks well before Fray Marcos stumbled into the mission at Tampico. It's known that on June 4, 1554, the viceroy in Mexico City allocated funds for a salvage mission under the command of Angel de Villafane to undertake a reconnaissance of the coastline in an effort to locate the lost ships. Six vessels were prepared at Vera Cruz to be commanded by an experienced mariner named Garcia de Escalante Alvarado.

There are several scenarios that speculate how the Spanish officials in Vera Cruz first learned of the shipwrecks. The one that many historians support is that at the time of the shipwrecks, Antonio Corzo, the captain of the *San Andreas* remained in the area long enough to observe that his three sister vessels had not survived the storm incident and were presumed lost. The *San Andreas* herself was badly damaged and limped into Havana in a near sinking condition. Thus, the news would have reached Havana relatively quickly that three ships, laden with treasure, had been lost somewhere along the gulf coast. Another scenario may have had another vessel sailing the coast and spotting the sunken ships, then returning quickly to Vera Cruz with the news. At that point, the castaways may already have begun their trek along the beach. Either way, a salvage effort was launched. After all the varied archival information is analyzed it is believed that a total of 304 persons were aboard the three lost ships. Since historians believe that since the accounts of the 1544 shipwrecks were written well after the tragedy occurred, therefore the accounts would have been somewhat blurred, embellished, or were in some aspects in error in one way or another. As we have seen, the accounts of the survivors were patched together from various sources. What is known is that the survivors did attempt to trek from the Padre Island shipwreck sites to Vera Cruz, and few lived to tell the tale!

Sadler and the Fight for the Padre Island Treasure

After the Texas authorities forced the Platoro Group to cease salvage operations in the field, a new phase in the treasure saga began. The State of Texas had moved quickly to seize the treasure that had been transported to Gary, Indiana for conservation and safe-keeping. In response, Platoro prepared to go to court to recover the treasure that they believed was legally theirs. The State of Texas, in the guise of the General Land Office, maintained that because the treasure was recovered from state waters, that it automatically belonged to Texas. Platoro countered that position with their own argument; attorney John Stiles wrote, "Nothing in the Texas constitution or statutes specifically covered the granting of permits for a marine archaeological or salvage expedition such as the one that Platoro was engaged in."

After Platoro was enjoined from further salvage off Padre Island a period of negotiation and litigation began. On March 6, 1968, the Znika brothers and their legal counsel, John Stiles, met with the Texas Land Commissioner Jerry Sadler and his legal staff in Sadler's office. Also attending the meeting was Jack Giberson, a Land Commission official as well as a State of Texas Deputy Attorney General for Natural Resources. Also attending the meeting was Billy Kenon, along with Mendel Peterson, who had flown in from Washington D.C. to lend his support and expertise. The primary goal of the meeting was to work out an administrative and/or legal settlement and determine the ownership of the treasure, or who owned what portion of the treasure. In Florida, the state recognized, but regulated private ownership of treasure, but shared in the treasure trove through conducting periodic divisions of treasure — in other words, a partnership model!

At the meeting, Mendel Peterson was prepared to relate that Platoro had followed all of the standard guidelines, both in their fieldwork and in the conservation laboratory in Gary, Indiana. Since Billy Kenon knew more about the fieldwork he was prepared to explain in detail both the remote sensing methodology as well as the excavation procedures that had been performed in murky waters off Padre Island. It was Billy's opinion that the state officials were much more interested in the administrative-legal issues concerning the project than they were in learning or understanding the ground-breaking work performed by the Platoro Group and their shipwreck excavation and conservation efforts.

Negotiations continued through the spring and summer of 1968; it appeared that some progress toward an amicable resolution of the conflict might be reached. In the fall, October 10, 1968, Jerry Sadler traveled to Gary, Indiana to examine the artifacts and treasure. Although Platoro was legally enjoined from returning to, or salvaging the site, Billy Kenon believes that the *Espiritu Santo* had been almost completely salvaged at the time that Platoro was forced to cease field operations. Although the State of Texas would later continue the archaeological excavation of the site under the direction of archaeologists Carl J. Clausen and J. Barto Arnold, the records show that no significant amount of treasure was recovered in three post-Platoro seasons. These later salvage seasons directed by the State of Texas archaeologists will be examined more closely later.

On November 12, 1968, the Znika brothers, Billy Kenon and counsel Stiles returned to the Texas State Capitol at Austin believing that a written agreement would be signed that would allow Platoro to resume salvage off Padre Island. From the time that Platoro was enjoined from further salvage, until the time of the November meeting, the State of Texas, General Land Office, and Commissioner Sadler had prepared rules and regulations dealing with the issuance of permits for marine archaeological excavations and had prepared a tentative agreement for Platoro and their legal counsel, John Stiles to examine. On December 18, a final form of the contract was sent from Sadler's office to the Platoro Group; the contract was then signed by Platoro and returned to the General Land Office for their signatures. At this point, it looked as though an agreement was in the works, but as time would tell, in the treasure business — looks could be deceiving!

In an act of good faith, and to show his professional support, Mendel Peterson, the Platoro archaeological consultant attended some of the meetings with Commissioner Sadler. Peterson agreed with the recommendation that there was a need for rules and regulations for underwater archaeological investigations, and stated yet again on the record to Commissioner Sadler that, "the search and recovery methods of Platoro were consistent with a quality marine archaeological investigation." Peterson, from his office at the Smithsonian Institution, had been following the State of Florida treasure salvage problem with more than passing interest; although there had been some administrative bumps in the road Peterson believed that the State of Florida and the Real Eight Group of treasure hunters had forged a stable win-win relationship that allowed treasure hunters and state regulators to work together.

At this point, it appeared that an agreement was near. On December 23, 1968, Commissioner Sadler wrote a letter to Platoro and enclosed newspaper articles describing news conferences that he (Sadler) had called where he exhibited some artifact material that Platoro had returned, and also that a contract had been entered into between Commissioner Sadler's office and the Platoro Group. The nuts and bolts details of the agreement as stated by Sadler were simple and to the point; there would be a 50/50 division of artifacts between the State of Texas and the Platoro Group, and Platoro would be allowed to return to the field under the same division of artifacts agreement once the final contract document was signed. In actuality, the contract had already been prepared and sent to Platoro Attorney John Stiles. In turn, Stiles and Platoro agreed with the contract as negotiated, signed it and then returned the contract to Commissioner Sadler. The contract was never signed by Commissioner Sadler, and that final and binding contract copy was never returned to the Platoro Group attorney, John Stiles. This whole on-again, off-again behavior on the part of Sadler was unsettling to all involved and would eventually become the administrative undoing of Commissioner Sadler.

As time went by and Commissioner Sadler bought his office additional time, storm clouds were gathering on the horizon. Certain members of the Texas State Legislature, likely at the behest of academic institutions and the historic preservation lobby began to question the tentative contract that had been proposed between Sadler's office and the Platoro Group. Legislators also maintained that The General Land Office had no jurisdiction in the area of historic preservation and shipwreck salvage, and on their own behalf argued that specific Antiquities Legislation should be passed that dealt with the preservation of historic shipwreck resources in Texas State waters.

Jerry Sadler also saw the proverbial writing on the wall. In the face of the growing political controversy, the commissioner began to drag his feet to buy time and failed to release to Platoro a final signed copy of the negotiated agreement. Attorney John Stiles in the summer of 1969 wrote describing the communication between the two parties during this tenuous period: "He (Sadler) continually assured Platoro's attorney that the Platoro Group did have a signed contract and that the Attorney General would dismiss the pending suit, as soon as Platoro was ready to return to the field and resume salvage operations."

In April 1969 the Texas State Legislature began to hold hearings in Austin with the ultimate goal of passing legislation that would protect historic shipwreck resources. Mendel Peterson testified at these hearings and again spoke favorably of the Platoro Group's archaeological salvage efforts. Commissioner Jerry Sadler also had to testify that he had a contract in the works with Platoro that, once signed, would allow Platoro to renew field operations. This was certainly anathema to the Texas cultural lobby of academics, politicians, and administrators alike. Still, there was no doubt that Sadler believed that his office had control over State of Texas submerged lands. He probably regretted offering an olive branch to Platoro, while at the same time he was likely impressed with how much treasure Platoro had recovered. By stringing Platoro along with the carrot and stick approach of a state-approved salvage contract, Sadler had affected the return of some of the treasure. It may have been that Sadler believed that Texas was going to be the new improved Florida style treasure hunting state and that the General Land Office was competent to administer salvage contracts and manage an equitable division of artifacts.

Then Commissioner Sadler played another card, telling Platoro that they needed to return all of the treasure to the State of Texas before the suit (injunction) could be lifted allowing them to return to the field. In light of this request, Platoro cooperated, but not fully. According to Attorney Stiles, "Subsequently another sizable shipment was made, but some of the artifacts (treasure) were retained because of Platoro's concern as to whether the Texas Attorney General would cooperate with the General Land Office as was being represented to us by Mr. Sadler."

Then Jerry Sadler realized that by offering Platoro a deal he had made a mistake. Sadler underestimated the power of the emerging purist archaeological and historic preservation community and their deeply felt belief that private groups and individuals had no business owning and dealing in historic shipwreck artifacts. Sadler, as Commissioner of the General Land Office, was both a politician and an administrator, with a foot in both the political and bureaucratic environments. Billy Kenon believed that Sadler ultimately saw that there was power and revenue for his office if he was allowed to administer a salvage program as had been constituted in Florida, but that he also had to deal with and placate the preservationist community. Quickly he came to understand that the preservationist movement constituted a very powerful lobby that influenced voters as well as elected representatives sitting in the State House in Austin. Sadler then became a preservationist himself, distancing himself from the regulated free-market position he had taken when he offered Platoro the possibility of a contract and a 50/50 split of artifacts.

At this point in the controversy, Commissioner Sadler decided to become an author. It was in about 1969 or 1970 that Sadler wrote a booklet entitled, *Treasure Tempest in Texas.* The booklet is interesting on a number of counts, first, there is no date of publication, and no publisher cited in the booklets first pages. By all appearances, Sadler published the booklet through the General Land Office. Throughout the book, Sadler refers to himself in the third person as 'Commissioner Sadler' and throughout the publication, he touted himself as a diligent public watchdog who was only trying to save the Padre Island treasure for the "School Children of Texas". There is only the most minor reference to the possibility that Platoro might be awarded a contract by the state. Even here Sadler suggests that he knew that Platoro, although attempting to come into compliance, never would. In his *Treasure Tempest in Texas* publication, Sadler writes, "The final contract was received by the General Land Office on March 28, 1969, but it never became effective because the Commissioner has never finally approved and signed the agreement."

In *Treasure Tempest in Texas* Sadler offers his version of the whistleblowing incident (sans Jeff Burke) that brought the state agents down on Platoro. Sadler writes, "An employee of the General Land Office in the Port Isabel area investigated a treasure hunting operation off of Padre Island." Sadler contends that his agents interviewed Platoro divers, who confirmed that a salvage operation was underway. Sadler admits that upon hearing of the salvage that he formally requested that the State of Texas Attorney General enjoin Platoro from further work in the field. Nowhere in *Treasure Tempest in Texas* does Jerry Sadler offer, or admit, that he was attempting to work out a 50/50 treasure division with the Platoro Group; nor did he admit that he negotiated the contract in good faith.

Sadler later contended that a contract was in the works, but never finalized. After admitting that a contract had been in the works, he then seemed to back-track a bit, maintaining that to operate, and do business in Texas, the Platoro Group needed a charter, and that they never obtained such a charter, and again reiterated that the treasure had to be returned into the custody of the State of Texas before an agreement could be reached. Sadler writes, "Then came the long and ticklish negotiations and legal maneuvering by which Commissioner Sadler attempted and was ultimately successful in his efforts to return the treasures to Texas."

The return of the treasure to Texas as in the contract negotiations turned into an extended and drawn-out process. Platoro continued to hold out the belief that a final signed contract would allow Billy Kenon and the dive team to return to operations in the field. Platoro was also advised that they might have to return all the remaining treasure to the State of Texas if they were to have any chance of resuming field operations. Platoro Attorney John Stiles wrote in a project synopsis; "Platoro had retained a sizable portion of the recovered treasure in Gary, and in early June 1969, Sadler advised Platoro he would have to have delivery of the balance of the artifacts before the suit (injunction) could be dismissed and the contract released." Subsequently, another sizable shipment was made, but once again, some of the items were retained because of Platoro's concern as to whether the Texas Attorney general would cooperate with the General Land Office as was being represented to us by Commissioner Sadler.

Attorney John Stiles maintains that by retaining some of the treasure, Platoro was exerting extreme pressure on Commissioner Sadler who was constantly under scrutiny from Texas legislators and preservationist groups who wanted the treasure returned to Texas. Stiles maintains that by retaining the treasure that Platoro forced Sadler to show his true colors. Stiles writes, "Later in the summer (1969) the pressure became so extreme on Sadler that he disavowed the contract stating that there never had been a contract and that he only represented that there was a contract in order to make Platoro return all the artifacts to the State of Texas. In other words, Sadler publically admitted, that as a public official, he had purposely misled, if not defrauded Platoro to accomplish what the State had not accomplished in a court of law — the return of the Padre Island Treasure."

According to Sadler, there were three deliveries of treasure to his facility, the first in the days after Platoro was enjoined from any activity on the site, the second in December 1968, and another in June 1969. In *The Nautical Archaeology of Padre Island* (Arnold and Weddle), the story differs slightly: "In August 1969 the State of Texas archaeologist, Curtis Tunnell and two Texas rangers made another trip to Indiana where they recovered yet another portion of treasure." Quickly there was the formation of a special committee to take inventory of the treasure for the State and then ensure that the collection was properly and professionally conserved. Eventually, all of the treasure came under the administration of Dr. W.W. Newcomb of the Texas Memorial Museum in Austin.

In the *Treasure Tempest in Texas* publication, Commissioner Sadler has another account of the treasures return to Texas. According to Sadler, "On December 18, 1968, two field-men from the Land Office drove to Indiana and returned with a footlocker full of treasure, and with assurances from Platoro that the locker contained all of the items which had been recovered and processed." These were most probably the valuable astrolabes and silver coins. During this same period, contract negotiations were underway, Sadler wanted all of the artifacts returned before a contract could be issued. Sadler writes, "Repeated telephone calls to Platoro failed to get the treasures started back to Texas." Tired of excuses Sadler returned his agents to Gary, Indiana where eventually two truckloads — all the remaining artifacts — were returned to safekeeping in Austin. Sadler takes all the credit writing, "And on that day, Commissioner Sadler remained the only man in Texas who had made any effort whatever to retrieve the treasures and bring them back to Texas."

While Commissioner Sadler bought time negotiating with Platoro, the Texas State Legislature was addressing the issue of protecting archaeological sites and sunken cultural resources in state waters. In September of 1969, a Texas State Antiquities Code was voted into law; there was no doubt that Platoro had been the lightning rod for this legislation. The newly enacted code required the establishment of an antiquities committee that would control and supervise the salvage and excavation of prehistoric and historic artifacts from state lands, including pre-twentieth-century shipwrecks found on the tidelands. As a result of this legislation, Judge Martineau directed on September 24, 1969, that the entire assemblage of treasure be placed in the temporary custody of the Texas Archaeological Research Laboratory known as TARL at the University of Texas, Austin. The treasure of the *Espiritu Santo* consisted of a number of aforementioned categories of artifacts; there was the treasure to be sure, gold and silver bullion, gold and silver coins, extremely early and valuable astrolabe navigation instruments, the iron guns along with other items of cargo that included ship's rigging and ballast stones. Later in this book a description and analysis of the Padre Island treasure will confirm the pioneer underwater archaeology work that the Platoro Group carried out at Padre Island.

Spanish Salvage Efforts at Padre Island

Soon, after word of the shipwrecks reached Vera Cruz both waterborne and land-bound expeditions were organized and departed for the shipwreck site. The land expedition that would travel north along the coastline was organized, commanded by an adventurer named Angel de Villafane whose background as a soldier in the wars against the Aztecs in Central Mexico prepared him and his troops for the arduous march along the coast. Villafane began his expedition with a general destination in mind, the coast of La Florida, near the Rio de Las Palmas at 26 and ½ degrees. The information that the wreck was close to the Rio de Las Palmas was in error; the river is some 165 nautical miles south of the shipwreck site. The latitude at 26 degrees was found to be accurate within eight miles; this leads one to believe that after the shipwrecks a competent navigator took a celestial reading at the disaster site, then perhaps a small boat took this information to Vera Cruz. This discrepancy can be attributed to the primitive cartography of the day, and a failure to understand the locations of key features along the coast.

Once the story of shipwreck reached Mexico the tale of the relief expedition becomes complicated. It would have taken some time for the official relief and salvage expedition to organize and depart Vera Cruz, however, more opportunistic salvage expeditions were launched almost immediately. The Mayor of Panuco acting as the agent for the renegade salvors who rushed to the shipwreck sites recovered a substantial 4,305 marks of silver and an additional 2,302 pesos of shipwreck treasure. When Villafane, traveling along the shoreline, arrived at Panuco, the first opportunistic salvors had already returned with booty. It is uncertain if this recovered treasure was meant to be shared among the initial raiders or returned to the Royal Treasury in Vera Cruz. It is likely that the salvaged treasure would not have been declared, and gone into the pantaloons of the brigands. As the story goes, Villafane confiscated all of the treasure that he intercepted, then had a party return with it to Vera Cruz, while his larger party continued on the trek to the shipwreck sites.

The slower waterborne, Garcia de Escalante Alvarado salvage, was launched from Vera Cruz on July 15, and 102 men on six vessels arrived at the shipwreck site on July 22. The day of arrival was auspicious; July 22 was the Catholic Magdalens Day, and thereafter cartographers utilized the term the Costa de Madalens, or Magdalen's Coast, and Medanos (sandbank) de Madalena for the present Padre Island coastline. No doubt in their imaginations they expected to see the haunting and gut-wrenching sight of the three vessels stranded in the shallows, their decks awash, and masts and sails either missing or hanging in disarray. The only vessel that remained visible above water was the *San Esteban*, the northernmost of the sites. After closer examination of the area, Alvarado determined that the sites were laid out as follows; the *Santa Maria De Yciar* was the southernmost wreck, the middle wreck was the *Espiritu Santo* and the northernmost wreck was the *San Esteban*. The *Santa Maria De Yciar* was located near the mouth of the present-day Port Mansfield Channel, and as a viable wreck site has been lost to posterity.

The land-bound Villafane expedition reached the site a day before the Alvarado vessels arrived. Villafane had brought native divers along on the trek, but without boats, he would have been limited to working from the beach. The initial salvage was carried out on the *San Esteban*, the northernmost wreck that was visible above water; this was the vessel that the rogue salvors who had arrived earlier from Panuco had salvaged. Since only one shipwreck could be seen with any exposed superstructure, Villafane and Alvarado conferred at the salvage encampment and decided that Villafane would take the pilot boat and a crew to search for the other two vessels by dragging a grappling hook. With the search for the other two vessels underway Alvarado began the salvage of the *San Esteban*. It is not documented in the archives as to how the salvage was performed but the probable methodology is easy to reconstruct. A small boat would have been tethered to the side of the *San Esteban*, the upper-deck of which might have been visible above water. Often stranded vessels with a portion of their upper hulls visible would be burned to the water-line exposing the ships hold and cargo area; this was not the case with the *San Esteban*. The amount of deck remaining and the amount of the vessel visible above water would dictate how entry into a flooded hold would be carried out.

Once the below-deck area and hold were exposed then ladders could be placed and a crew could enter the hold and affix hooks and ropes to chests and crates of treasure and other valuable cargo, then haul the goods to the surface, and lower the salvaged cargo into a small cutter. When it came to diving on a shipwreck site the Spanish would usually use native Indian divers. The Indian pearl divers from Venezuela were considered the most adept divers; however coastal Amerindians from throughout the Americas also made excellent salvage divers. Since the natives dove and fished for food, they were skilled in the water whereas Europeans tended not to be swimmers, nor even to have an affinity with washing or bathing.

A skilled native diver could hold his breath for several minutes and once entering a flooded ship's hold would tie ropes to chests and place loose material into bags that were then pulled to the surface. Outside of the divers brought from Mexico by Villafane, it seems that, contrary to the norm, some divers, were in fact, Spanish seamen; the archives described one as pilot and diver, and also that he was illiterate. Perhaps this individual had been born poor in the New World and would have been one of the early Mexican colonial class; his status was also elaborated by the fact that he could neither read nor write. Pilots had varying skills, some knew local waters intimately, and were able to steer vessels into tricky or difficult harbor entrances like modern harbor pilots. Others were more adept at taking on new voyages of discovery, and possessed the sixth sense of a natural-born sailor. Many pilots were well educated and literate, and as open water mariners wrote "rutters", small books on navigation routes, descriptions of harbors, bathymetry, and routes into difficult harbors, bays, and inlets.

The salvage was concluded on September 12, 1554. All of the recovered treasure had been stacked in piles on the beach; it must have been an imposing sight. The precious metals, coins and bullion, and other valuables were recorded and weighed by royal officials. The bullion from the *San Esteban* was calculated at 9,000 pesos in coin while the *Espiritu Santo*'s salvage amounted to 11,000 pesos, and the *Santa Maria de Yciar* treasure amounted to 2,000 pesos in coin. By this calculation, the salvage totaled 29,078 pounds of silver bullion and 22,000 pesos.

Alvarado ordered the treasure loaded on the brigantine *Mendoza* and dispatched the vessel down the coast for San Juan de Ulua. At San Juan, the treasure was off-loaded to barges for the short trip to Vera Cruz and was then transferred ashore at the mouth of the

Rio Vera Cruz. The treasure was then unloaded at the wharf, weighed, and transferred to a nearby stone building where a wine cellar was cleared so the treasure could be stored securely pending shipment to Havana, and then on to Spain.

In the chaos of treasure salvage, there was always the problem of thievery. After the salvaged treasure was removed from the *Mendoza* the vessel was thoroughly searched and caches of treasure were found hidden throughout the vessel. The total came to 624 marks of silver (312 pounds) and 600 pesos in coin, calculated in modern value to $26,000. In treasure salvage, necessity was the mother of invention and even the representatives of the Spanish Crown were not above stealing what they believed to be their share of the shipwreck spoils.

The final tally of the recovered treasure from the 1554 ship-wrecks was computed from all of the combined salvage efforts, those of *Mendoza's* crew, the people of Panuco, along with the Villafane and Alvarado land and sea forays to Padre Island. In the end the *San Esteban* salvage computed to a weight of 14,944 pounds of treasure that included silver coins and bullion. The *Espiritu Santo* wreck yield-ed 14,635 pounds, 26,897 marks of silver and 11,000 pesos of gold. Of approximately 15,000 pounds of treasure registered on the *Santa Maria de Yciar*, approximately 6,225 were recovered, including 2,000 pesos in coin. The total weight of the salvaged treasure tallied to 35,804 pounds. Without the manifests of the *San Esteban* and *Espiritu Santo*, there appears to be no reliable method of determining how much gold and silver the three vessels carried, to begin with. In the absence of reliable tonnage figures, it must be assumed that each ship's size was roughly proportionate to the value of the cargos she had brought from Spain. On that basis, the *Santa Maria de Yciar* must have been consid-erably smaller than her two sister ships. From the manifest of the *San Andres*, the vessel that avoided shipwreck at Padre Island, we know that she carried more than two and one-half times as much treasure as that registered on *Santa Maria de Yciar*.

Perhaps, then, it is not going too far afield to assume that the proportion of salvage from the other two ships in relation to the amount they carried was about the same as that of *Santa Maria de Yciar*, about forty-one percent. The total carried by the three vessels, therefore, would have been some 87,000 pounds. With 35,804 pounds recovered, some 51,331 remained lost, laying on the bottom of the Gulf awaiting eventual salvage. It is difficult to compute the value of the Padre Island treasure in contemporary terms; however, it is safe to say that it would have to be computed at many millions of dollars.

From the beginning of the historic salvage efforts, there were misgivings concerning the amount of treasure recovered. There were various conspiracy stories and tales woven about the immediate aftermath of the shipwrecks. Stories began to circulate that immediately after the tragedy, that the more opportunistic officers and seamen gathered the survivors together near one of the wrecks and then went to another of the wrecks, salvaged easily accessible treasure and buried it somewhere in the deep backshore sand dunes of Padre Island. Then there were the early forays from Panuco by semi-official treasure hunters as well as other freebooters. We do not know exactly where these treasure hunters worked first, or from which shipwreck they recovered their treasure. Would they have taken their booty directly back to Vera Cruz or buried it somewhere along the coastal sand-dunes and recovered it later?

Any number of unofficial treasure hunts were probably launched from Mexican ports to the site of the 1554 shipwrecks. These expeditions could have been carried out using boats as small as thirty or forty feet. The voyage up the coast to the shipwreck site could have been taken on the direct trajectory from Vera Cruz to Padre Island, or up the coast just offshore following the survivors' trek in reverse. There is no doubt that additional salvage took place and this treasure disappeared into the unwritten and undocumented realm of secret treasure trove. By contrast, at the 1715 shipwreck sites in Florida, the Spanish were able to manage at least three seasonal returns to the wrecks, then, over time, the sites were abandoned. Being near the Gulf Stream, this well-traveled shipping route would have brought ships of other nations to the sites, and periodic salvage would have continued. Gradually these sites faded into the realm of legend, and only annotations on old maps suggested that treasure might still be found in offshore shallows. It is impossible to determine how much treasure has been recovered, from colonial times to contemporary times, along both the Padre Island shoreline and the Florida Treasure Coast.

Final Accounting for Platoro

In response to the loss of all the salvaged treasure to the State of Texas, and denial by Jerry Sadler that a working contract existed between the Platoro Group and the state, Attorney Stiles, at the direction of the Znika brothers, filed a Federal salvage claim on August 6, 1969, in the United States District Court in Brownsville, Texas. Since Platoro attorney Stiles was not licensed to practice law in Texas and was not by legal specialization an admiralty attorney, it was decided to retain the firm of Hardy and Sharp, a well-known and respected law firm that had the expertise to litigate and deliver a fair decision for Platoro. Although the new Platoro attorneys were comfortable with the Brownsville legal venue, this was soon to become a problem.

It took two years due to a series of legal motions and continuances, for the case to finally reach the courtroom. On November 1st and 2nd, 1973, a trial was held in the U.S. Federal Court testing the merits of Platoro's case. Mendel Peterson testified before Judge Reynaldo G. Garza that the monetary value of the salvaged treasure that had largely been recovered by Kenon and a handful of divers amounted to $294,618. Judge Garza accepted Peterson's expert testimony without question and ruled that the amount that Platoro would be awarded would be one half of that amount, less some artifact conservation costs. The Texas State Archaeologist Curtis Tunnell and Commissioner Sadler did not agree with Peterson's evaluation; however, Judge Garza overruled their objections.

Finally, on December 26, 1973, the Federal Court at Brownsville awarded Platoro $131, 248. Out of this award, Platoro was directed to pay $8,750 to Jefferson T. Burke, and $3,000 to Billy Algoe. Jeff Burke was identified as the disaffected whistleblower and crop-duster pilot, and Algoe had in fact worked for Platoro as a deckhand but believed that he had been short-changed in the settlement.

Judge Garza also warned that if the State of Texas did not pay Platoro within a reasonable amount of time that portions of the treasure, in state custody, would be awarded to the Platoro Group to satisfy the judgment. In the end, Judge Garza, having read the background of the case, and the fact that Commissioner Sadler had made a tentative contract offer to split the treasure, 50/50, agreed that the State of Texas would be awarded half of the $294,618.

But the legal fight was not over. Like quicksilver the decision slipped away as the State of Texas filed another appeal, this time in the 5th Circuit Court of Appeals in New Orleans. This appeal was based on an issue of jurisdiction. Platoro attorney John Stiles has written a clear explanation of what occurred. Simply stated, at the time that the suit was filed by Platoro the treasure had been returned from Gary, Indiana to Texas, and was stored at the University of Texas in Austin for conservation and restoration. The jurisdictional issue centered on the fact that the treasure was stored in Austin, and not Brownsville. The appeals judge ruled that the Platoro lawsuit should have been filed in Brownsville. In hindsight, John Stiles believed that by acting in good faith and willingly returning the treasure to Texas, that a tactical mistake had been made, a mistake that would take additional time and litigation to correct. Attorney Stiles wrote: "Such was the ruling, even though the site of the discovery of the shipwrecks and the salvage took place in the jurisdiction of the Southern District Federal Court. Platoro's willingness to cooperate with the state in order to ensure preservation had been a tactical mistake." It appears that if Platoro had simply stored the artifacts in some warehouse in Brownsville, and allowed them to deteriorate, their victory in the Federal Court in Brownsville would have been upheld. Attorney Stiles wrote, "The venue question may best be described as nonsense — not Justice."

However, the Federal Appeals Court in New Orleans that had overturned the Garza decision gave Billy a ray of hope in the face of the controversial Brownsville vs Austin, venue decision. Written into the Federal Appeals Court decision was the opinion that the State of Texas would have to pass a bill to allow Billy Kenon and Platoro to sue. Billy and Platoro then contacted State Representative Rene Olivera who agreed to introduce the legislation. To make a long story short the bill was introduced and summarily defeated. At that point Billy faced a dilemma, to continue his fight for a fair ending to the case, or throw in the towel. Billy went to Platoro to gain their support and some funding. Platoro said that they were finished — Billy was on his own!

It was now 1975 and Billy decided to push ahead with his case alone. Billy contacted a prominent lawyer in Brownsville, Texas named

Jack Sanchez and asked him for advice. The Sanchez family had been friends with the Kenon family for years, and Jack Sanchez advised Billy to go to the State capital in Austin and start to contact state represen-tatives and convince them of the merits of his case. When Billy ar-rived in Austin he began to make the rounds of legislators — both state representatives and senators. One of Billy's primary targets was Jack Bingham the representative from Freeport, Texas who had teamed up with Commissioner Sadler to lead the long and vindictive fight against Plataro. For weeks Billy and Bingham played a drawn-out game of 'cat and mouse', where Billy went to Bingham's office and Bingham would allegedly not be in. When Billy attempted to collar Bingham in a hall-way, the representative was surrounded by a phalanx of staffers, and on the way to a hearing. Finally, Billy and Bingham met — both tired of the chase! Billy in his low-key business-like manner sat down with Bingham and told him his side of the Padre Island shipwreck salvage story. Bingham listened intently and asked Billy a series of probing questions that offered some balance to the one-sided Commissioner Sadler version of the Padre Island saga. The outcome of the Kenon-Bingham dialogue was a milestone in Billy's quest for justice. Bingham advised Billy to get his own state representative re-involved, and that he (Bingham) would support Billy's quest to sue the State of Texas.

In order to get the bill on the legislative docket, Billy had to attend and testify at a series of legislative hearings, largely on his own. This process was time-consuming and costly, taking hundreds of hours and thousands of dollars. Finally, after Billy had jumped through all the legislative hoops, Representative Rene Olivera and Representative Jack Bingham wrote and introduced the new legislation. Although it sounds hard to believe, the legislation passed both the Texas, House of Representatives, and State Senate. Billy's attorney, Jack Sanchez, then filed suit to allow Billy to finally sue the State of Texas and recover the full value of the Padre Island treasure.

The suit was filed and like clockwork Billy lost again. Refusing to give up, Billy went to court at least six more times, over as many years, at a personal cost of approximately $200,000 dollars. Eventually, the Sanchez Law Firm fees would reach $90,000 dollars, a small amount of the money that Sanchez actually spent in his pursuit of justice for Plataro. The bottom line was that the pursuit of justice in the courts had become a lifestyle for Billy Kenon; this did not mean that Billy spent every waking hour seeking justice, but the case was almost always on his mind and draining money from his wallet. When Billy met the Znika brothers he was a young salvor and over the two decades of litigation he had married, fathered three children, divorced, and married again wedding his present wife and partner Esther, who manages his office in Port Isabel.

In 1989 the case went to the Federal Admiralty Court in Odessa, Texas with Judge Button presiding. It had been twenty years since September 12, 1967, when Billy Kenon and his team found the first treasure off of Padre Island and this hearing in Odessa, Texas would almost be an anti-climax to the case. At this hearing, Judge Button awarded Billy $294,000, or one hundred percent of the value of the treasure plus interest. Of course, the State of Texas appealed; by this time Platoro had re-entered the case and assumed some of Billy's out of pocket expenses during all the appeals by the State of Texas.

The next phase of the litigation took place in the Federal 5th Circuit Court in New Orleans, where a panel of judges presided. This time the writing was on the wall; remember Judge Button had already found for Kenon when he presided in Odessa, Texas. And perhaps the State of Texas was concerned about the amount of taxpayer dollars spent on the case; these expenditures counted in the millions and included the litigation against Platoro, as well as the three years of state salvage after Platoro had been enjoined from working on the site.

In the end, the court's decision appeared to find an equitable outcome to the long and rancorous struggle between Platoro and the State of Texas. It was the court's decision that the State of Texas would be awarded all the treasure and artifacts, and Billy and the Znika brothers would be awarded the $294,618 with interest. Billy Kenon was not happy with the dollar amount of the award that was based on the initial appraisal of the treasure Mendel Peterson had initially made in court. Billy Kenon respected Peterson as a professional but believed that as a conservative archaeologist, Peterson would not have been comfortable placing a high monetary value on the Padre Island artifact and treasure assemblage. Archaeologists view artifacts and the precious metals that are labeled as treasure as objects where the historic/cultural value is, of course, high, but it is almost immoral to view shipwreck artifacts as having a monetary or collector value. Kenon agrees that the Platoro legal team would have been better served if they had gone to the private sector and retained a qualified antiquities professional from an auction house like Christie's or Sotheby's to appraise the treasure. Also, the coins that were recovered should have been appraised by an experienced professional coin appraiser, a numismatist, who would have placed a high value on these early coins from New Spain.

It appeared as if the saga of the Padre Island shipwreck salvage was coming to a close. It would not be a completely successful end as Billy saw it, but at least there might be an outside chance that Texas would adopt a shipwreck salvage program similar to Florida's, where he would be able to search for historic shipwrecks in Texas waters or even return to the Padre Island shipwreck sites. But this was not to be — the State of Texas returned to court and appealed the Garza judgment.

In the final accounting, the $294,618 plus interest was divided into four fairly equitable parts; the Sanchez law firm that had stepped up and taken the case was awarded $90,000; Platoro $80,000; Billy, $85,000 and the two other members of Billy's salvage crew, Purvis and Algoe, split another $85,000. In the end, Billy considered his payout to be very little for his time and effort spent fighting the state, and then the final blow to Billy's interests and aspirations was the sad fact that Texas wanted nothing to do with administering a controversial salvage program as had been adopted in Florida.

In a "Brownsville Herald" story published on June 19, 1984, the headline read, 'Platoro treasure dispute settled'. The story is important because it encapsulates all of the Platoro odyssey in about five hundred words. The settlement differs a bit as reported elsewhere, but states that Billy Kenon and George Purvis would receive a sum of $313,000; the article states that, "The award is nearly triple the amount the company would have received under a federal court ruling in 1973 before it was overturned by the 5th U.S. Circuit Court of Appeals." The article reiterated that the State of Texas would retain custody of the treasure and that pending lawsuits would be dissolved.

The 1984 newspaper article also cited the fact that the Platoro salvage had prompted passage of the Texas Antiquities Code, banning the recovery sunken pre-20th century vessels within a 10-mile state waters territorial limit. The article also excoriated the handling of the case by Jerry Sadler of the General Land Office, who by 1984 had passed away. The "Brownsville Herald" article states that the Texas Antiquities Code was... "Passed largely because of the public uproar over the salvage and the handling of the case by the General Land Office. The dispute also contributed to Sadler's defeat in his bid for re-election as state land commissioner in 1970."

Dennis Sanchez of the Sanchez Law Firm of Brownsville was also quoted in the article. Dennis Sanchez was the younger brother of Jack Sanchez who had gone to bat for Billy Kenon after the Hardy & Sharpe firm completed their earlier litigation on the behalf of Platoro. Showing how long the case had been drawn out the Brownsville newspaper article pointed out that Attorney Dennis Sanchez was only 15 years old when Billy Kenon located the *Espiritu Santo* in 1967. Dennis Sanchez also had a few words to say about the valuation of the treasure stating, "Realistically, if it was sold on the open market, it would go for about $500,000." Sanchez also disagreed with an estimate of the treasure's value that had been made by the late, Jerry Sadler; Sanchez called an earlier Sadler estimate of the Platoro treasure at $4.2 million dollars as — "sensationalistic."

In 1983, the year before the settlement an article appeared in a periodical named "The Armadillo". The article by Ray Nelson is titled, 'Are Finders Really Keepers', and discusses the Padre Island treasure controversy in down-home and folksy language. Nelson writes about a lunch with Billy Kenon and his family in a Port Isabel seafood restaurant. Nelson writes, "Well those politicians apparently didn't recognize a true native son, Billy has had them in court for the past 14 years and to date, he has won two favorable opinions." Nelson captures Billy's fighting spirit over sweet tea and a fish sandwich, "It's just that the state uses the taxpayer's money to appeal on technicalities and hope they can outlast me, Billy laughed softly." Nelson captures Billy's logic when Kenon says that, "They say they are confiscating the treasure for the public, but how many silver coins can they display? Do you know how many cannon are rusting in their storehouses?" Kenon summed up his position with the final salvos, "It's a case of state socialism versus private enterprise."

It had become apparent that Texas was not going to go the way of Florida! The State of Florida had regulated treasure hunting from the beginning of the Real Eight Corporation's discoveries in Florida, and over time the regulatory bureaucracy had grown along with the treasure hunting industry. However, at the national level the academic, anthropology and archaeology interests had taken a firm stand against relic and treasure hunting and of course, at the State level, these college and university interests had the political power to initiate and support preservationist interests nationwide. At the federal, state, and local level all of the government agencies that controlled government lands such as the Department of the Interior, and the Bureau of Land Management, joined with State agencies to prohibit treasure hunting on public lands. During the past decade UNESCO, the United Nations, Educational, Social and Cultural Organization has led the preservationist movement at the international level in an attempt to ban treasure hunting.

Friends In High Places

In parallel with all of the Platoro litigation work Billy also attempted to involve high visibility political candidates in his efforts to create a role for private sector salvage in Texas. Billy will admit that he was unsuccessful in these efforts. Billy initiated a conversation with George W. Bush at a Texas Shrimpers Association annual meeting. Billy politely presented his case, Bush listened but was noncommittal. In reality, it would not have been in the best interests of a Texas political candidate to support a private sector salvage company when the political (preservationist) movement was gaining strength.

Billy never had any success with Texas politicians in his attempt to get a hearing for responsible treasure hunting. Years later, Billy wrote another letter, this time, on the behalf of the shrimpers association to Senator Ted Cruz. Maybe if Cruz would respond to a hot political issue like free trade, and the Cheap Vietnamese shrimp imports that had been flooding onto the American market from South East Asia, perhaps he would be amenable to listening to what had happened to Platoro. No luck — Cruz apparently wasn't interested in fair trade and the American shrimpers. Cruz sent him a "thank you for your interest form letter."

In 1984, Texas Senator Lloyd Bentsen weighed into the shipwreck controversy in the "Brownsville Herald" article titled, 'Bentsen bill seeks to end treasure ship plundering.' You might remember that Bentsen was the candidate for VP on the Michael Dukakis ticket when Dukakis and Bentsen ran unsuccessfully against George H.W. Bush and Dan Quayle in the 1988 presidential election. In that memorable debate, Quayle attempted to compare his time spent in congress with that of former President, John F. Kennedy! Bentsen cut Quayle off at the knees with the snide comment, "Congressman Quayle, you're no Jack Kennedy." The Bentsen article is full of words like "plunder" and "looters", and Bentsen's goals and strategy are clear. What Bentsen proposed was to take historic shipwreck sites completely out of any private sector salvage; the Bentsen Bill introduced in the U.S. Congress would, "remove from maritime salvage provisions any shipwrecks eligible for inclusion on the National Register of Historic Places." The thrust of the Bentsen sponsored legislation was intended to close the loophole provided by Federal Admiralty Law; Barto Arnold was quoted as saying that, "Salvage firms have learned that they can legally get around the Texas Antiquities Law and plunder sunken treasure troves by going into federal court and winning lawsuits based on salvage provisions of maritime law which supersede state laws."

There was also the basic economic question of whether or not historic shipwreck salvage was a cost-effective enterprise. It would take another volume to explore the cost/benefit analysis issues that surround treasure hunting projects. The most recent cases of large salvage operations that have utilized remotely operated vehicles (ROVs) in the deepwater environment, and have recovered large cargos of treasure, like the *S.S. Central America* salvage in the deep Atlantic have recovered immensely valuable cargos, but ultimately become mired in both criminal and civil issues. In the "Brownsville Herald" article, State Archaeologist Barto Arnold weighs in on the Padre Island, Platoro Group salvage, making the point that although the monetary value of the treasure cargo was modest ($165,000), "cannons, anchors, ships fittings and other artifacts removed from the galleons — had very little monetary value, but very great historical and archaeological significance." This 1984 article also takes a swipe at Jerry Sadler and his attempt to carve out an on-again, off-again contract with Platoro. Hindsight is

20/20, and Sadler's contract, a copy of which was issued to Platoro, back-fired in the face of the state legislators and bureaucrats rejection of any deal with the Znika brothers and Billy Kenon. Remember, Texas never went the way of Florida, no deals with treasure hunters have ever been made. The "Brownsville Herald" article summed up the status of the case in 1984, "A court battle revolving around an alleged contract let by snuff-dipping former Land Commissioner Jerry Sadler — continues even today, with attorneys for Platoro saying they are close to an agreement on a salvage fee for raising the artifacts."

No doubt Mel Fisher would have a different take on the plight of Platoro and the question, "does treasure pay?" Mel would have set up a museum, a gift shop, and a restaurant on Padre Island and paraded the tourists through, as he did in Key West and Sebastian, Florida. Mel figured out what to do with all the coins recovered, he sold them as numismatic specimens to coin collectors and the marginally valuable as jewelry, pendants, and earrings. The treasure museum itself was a revolving door where the sun-burned and the bored were offered a brief respite from tacky souvenir and T-shirt shops!

The Replica Coin Problem

Since Platoro would not be physically awarded any of the treasure or artifacts the court offered Platoro the right to make reproductions of some of the treasure. This attempt to give Platoro, just a taste of treasure, amounted to what can only be described as a 'booby prize'. What would Platoro do with replicas — sell them as souvenirs, or establish their own museum full of reproductions? The stipulations that Platoro had to follow were clear and straightforward. Platoro could have 100 replicas made of a small rosary cross and one astrolabe. Additionally, at their option, Platoro could have 100 replicas of a selected coin, or instead of that, an additional payout of $5,000. Also, they could make five replicas of one small silver disc, or the small gold bar.

Replica coins had caused problems in the past and would cause more problems in the future. Treasure hunter entrepreneurs in Florida had made replica coins that were perhaps too authentic; some were so

Right: the reverse and obverse of a 4 reale recovered from the Esperitu Santo by the Platoro group. Known as a 'Pillars and Waves' design, this coin was minted in Mexico City. The assayer, noted on the obverse with the letter "P" was Pedro de Espina, assayer at the mint from 1538 - 1541.
Photos: Billy Kenon

good that only experienced coin dealers could tell a replica coin from a real coin. The treasure hunters selling replica coins were in no way attempting to deceive the buyer of the coin; they were generally sold in gift shops or jewelry stores as replicas and came with a certificate clearly stating that they were replica coins, but made from shipwreck silver. For example, a highly successful and famous treasure hunter found so many silver bars that he thought it was a good marketing idea to meltdown shipwreck bullion bars and make replica coins out of the silver. In other words, the silver was shipwreck silver, but the coins were replica coins. In a process disdained by museums and archaeologists, the top two inches of a silver bar, would be sawed off, and then the bar was melted down, and the reproduction coins were made. The top of the bar that had the important, and often visually stunning mint marks was then framed and marketed as a historic artifact. In a way this made sense to a treasure hunter entrepreneur; however stunning the mint marks were on the top of a silver bullion bar, it was difficult displaying such a heavy artifact, so the question was, why not preserve the coins numismatic information while utilizing the remaining shipwreck silver that could be made into hundreds or replica coins and jewelry. This process only opened the Pandora's Box of ethical issues. First, the sawing and melting process had defaced a historic artifact; then by trying to reproduce an authentic (but not too authentic) looking treasure coin, a fake coin had been made.

Within the reproduction agreement, the Texas Antiquities Committee attempted to insure that fake coins could not be reproduced; the authorities in Austin required that replicas would be made for personal use only, no commercial use would be possible; the reproduction coins could not be sold. Further, the replicas should have an outstanding technical and artistic quality and be made by a craftsman mutually agreeable to Platoro and the Antiquities Committee. The Antiquities Committee then made a final stipulation that "The replicas shall be individually numbered and marked to indicate that they are replicas of original artifacts owned by the State of Texas, as to which the State of Texas reserves all rights of reproduction." From the beginning, the replica coin scheme was a bad idea and Platoro never attempted to reproduce the 1554 type coins; in hindsight, this was a good decision on the part of Platoro.

Controlling the Shipwreck History

In the aftermath of the treasure salvage and confiscation of the treasure by the State of Texas, more infighting took place between Platoro and others who had worked, or thought they had contributed in some manner to the shipwreck project. Various groups had come to Padre Island, spent some time, and then lost interest and left. Jeff Burke from Rio Hondo who would consistently clash with the Znika brothers and Billy Kenon was the most notorious. In fact, Burke convinced one judge that he had hung around for enough time to be awarded a small percentage of the final settlement.

According to Billy, a group of treasure hunters from Florida led by Jack Haskins and John Potter was introduced to the Znika brothers by Jeff Burke during the early, remote sensing stage of the investigation. John Potter is well known as the author of *The Treasure Diver's Guide*. The book is a compendium of shipwreck history, bolstered by lists of shipwreck sites based on regional locations, like, The Gulf of Mexico and Yucatan, Florida, Bahamas, and Bermuda, etc. It is safe to say that no one ever discovered a shipwreck through the information in *The Treasure Diver's Guide*, however, the book does contain an extensive list of lost ships and general maritime history.

Jack Haskins, formally known as Goin E. Jack Haskins, was a treasure hunter from the Florida Keys. A self-proclaimed 'archives rat', Haskins had taught himself to read and translate colonial period Spanish script and had spent considerable time in the archives in Seville and Santo Domingo. In the early 1960s, Haskins had been on the hunt for the *Atocha* and *Santa Margarita* shipwrecks but was scooped by archivist-historian Eugene Lyon who beat Haskins to the punch providing Fisher with the archival information that led Fisher to the two shipwreck sites in the area of the Marquesas Keys. Haskins felt he was long overdue for a big shipwreck discovery. When Haskins and Potter heard about the Platoro Group's shipwreck theory, they made a bee-line for Padre Island!

In his section on the Padre Island shipwrecks, Potter documents the Platoro Group as the first treasure hunters on the Padre Island scene in the modern period of salvage. Potter writes, "Meanwhile a second venture headed by ex-UDT diver Jeff T. Burke, and Goin E. Jack Haskins, Jr., was at work." Potter continues, "The salvage reports made by the Spanish state that the ships were located near Rio de Las Palmas in 26 ½ degrees of latitude which would put them right near Port Mansfield." Haskins describes his role in the search for the shipwrecks, writing, "In the spring of 1968 Jeff Burke of Rio Hondo and I were able to locate all three of these ships using an ASQ-3 magnetometer. There can be no doubt from the evidence that we gathered that these ships are all sixteenth-century vessels and most probably the ones which carried the unfortunate three-hundred lost on Padre Island."

Billy Kenon remembers clearly the friction that took place during the early days of the search for the Padre Island shipwrecks, and Kenon maintains that he was in the field every day, and never saw Haskins or Potter in the field, especially during the critical period of the remote sensing survey. Further, the Rio Hondo Group, as far as he knew, never had any contractual standing in the project. It was true that Burke was in the field off and on and sometimes participated in the magnetometer surveys. Billy maintains that Burke's behavior of never being able to concentrate on one activity or take direction in the field, led to their eventual estrangement and the litigation that followed.

Eventually, the friction between Burke and the Platoro Group led to the intervention by the State of Texas, when Jeff Burke decided to go to the authorities. In his account of the litigation, Potter writes that "Haskins signed an affidavit that suggested where the shipwrecks were located. They had made (magnetometer) contacts at points three and a half and eight miles north of Port Isabel, about two and three miles south of Bob Hall Pier, and at several sites north of Port Mansfield Channel." In *The Treasure Divers Guide* Potter further relates that Haskins took the position that the salvage was made possible by their magnetometer search results. Paul Znika countered stating that Platoro had conducted their own magnetometer survey and had discovered the shipwrecks! Billy Kenon would stake his life on the fact that the Haskins–Potter crowd never discovered anything off Padre Island.

Potter also published several interesting tidbits in *The Treasure Divers Guide* that speaks to the venom that existed between the State of Texas and the Platoro Group. The first was a quote in 1969 from a Land Commissioner Jerry Sadler press-release. Sadler refers to Kenon and his fellows in the following vituperative prose: "Pilfering, plundering and pillaging pirates have looted the treasures of the lost ships. But we will catch them; we will find those pirates and bring them and their booty into a court of justice if we have to trail them around the world."

Potter did confirm the important fact that Jerry Sadler had made a contract with the Platoro Group, under whose terms fifty percent of the recoveries would be turned over to the State of Texas. Potter also confirmed that in January 1970 the attorney for Platoro (John Stiles) was quoted as saying that the state was interested in reaching an agreement for the 50/50 division of the treasure. Potter writes: "He (Stiles) was quickly contradicted by Assistant Attorney General Nola White", who was quoted as stating, "We want the whole hog. We think we're entitled to it. We think those people violated the law!"

The Padre Island Project Continues

At the time of the Padre Island shipwreck discoveries, the State of Texas Archaeologist was Curtis Tunnell, a 'dirt archaeologist' who had no underwater experience and knew very little about the newly emerging discipline of underwater archaeology. It was apparent that Tunnell was not going to be able to perform the fieldwork if the State of Texas intended to continue the Padre Island shipwreck project. Even today, some half-century after underwater archaeology has become an established academic discipline, there are few archaeologists that are comfortable working in both the underwater and terrestrial environments. After the State of Texas took over the Platoro sites they began to seek the services of an archaeologist who knew and understood the management of sunken cultural resources and also had experience with treasure salvage. The obvious choice was Carl Clausen, the underwater archaeologist who had developed and administered the State of Florida underwater treasure salvage program.

From 1964 until 1972 Clausen had been responsible for the field administration of the Florida salvage program. As described earlier, a fairly amicable administrative model had been worked out between the State of Florida, Kip Wagner, and his Real Eight Corporation. Wagner and his early cohorts were 'Gentleman Treasure Hunters', and during the early years of the salvage program, everyone seemed to get along with very little friction. However, over time as more sub-contractors began to work the Treasure Coast shipwrecks, and additional shipwrecks had been discovered, the State of Florida was forced to create a whole new agency devoted to both land and underwater archaeology; this became known as the Division of Historical Resources.

From the time that he was appointed the State of Florida Underwater Archaeologist, Clausen attempted to bring order to the Florida salvage program. One of Clausen's main concerns was that treasure hunters worked very quickly and did not seem to understand the slow, scientific, methodical, archaeological process where a grid is set up on a site, and the grids are excavated, one-by-one, in what is called a horizontal and vertical matrix. This meant that all artifacts at whatever level or position on a shipwreck could be recorded in situ (in place). The archaeologist would then, using the site plan and artifact positions, be able to analyze the site. This was often difficult when ship-wrecks were scattered and artifact locations spoke more to the physical dynamics of a shipwreck site, wave action and force of current, than to a more traditional, less disturbed site on land.

Also, in treasure hunting the old adage that time is money holds true. On the Florida Treasure Coast, there are only about 180 days of flat-water-weather when the prop-wash deflector boats could work in the dynamic nearshore environment. Most of the year there is a modest surf zone that precludes the anchoring of salvage vessels, and visibility on the bottom is poor.

This inability for the treasure hunters to understand the strict methodology was an irritant to Clausen, and there was always a tension within the salvage community. Clausen had been educated at the University of Florida in the anthropology department. His early work had been in pre-historic archaeology and he had made an important discovery at Little Salt Spring in Southwest Florida. In about 60 feet of water, resting on a submerged ledge, Clausen had discovered the slaughtered remains of an extinct turtle with a kill-shaft driven into its belly. Carbon 14 of associated charcoal material dated the site to 8,000 BCE, proving the early habitation of Florida by prehistoric peoples when sea levels were at their lowest and the turtle kill site was dry land.

Clausen accomplished a great deal as the state archaeologist and is considered a pioneer of underwater archaeology. Not only was Clausen the field administrator of the treasure salvage program, but he also developed a conceptual model of a 1715 shipwreck plan showing the ballast pile, cannons and anchors strewn over one hundred yards of sand, rock, and limestone reef ridges. All of the artifacts recovered were recorded on the site plans as they were discovered, and Clausen published the site plan in a book that he co-authored with Robert Burgess titled *Florida's Golden Galleons*. *Florida's Golden Galleons* was a follow-up to *Pieces of Eight* by Kip Wagner and L.B. Taylor, a pioneering history of the 1715 shipwreck salvage. Clausen's book was a well-written history of the treasure salvage business in Florida and documented the frustrations that Clausen had faced as both an archaeologist and an administrator.

The State of Texas 1972 Field Season

In 1972 Clausen left the employment of the State of Florida and migrated to Texas where he became the marine archaeologist with the State of Texas Historical Commission's Padre Island Underwater Archaeological Research Project. No doubt the Texas authorities saw Clausen as a person who could accomplish in Texas what he had done in Florida. As it turns out the Clausen Era in Texas was not to prove as congenial as anticipated.

According to Billy Kenon, when Clausen arrived in Texas in 1972 the Texas authorities had already traveled to Indiana to remove the remaining artifacts from the Platoro conservation facility, to return them to a conservation facility at the Texas Historical Society. The Arnold-Weddle, *Nautical History of Padre Island* volume states that in July 1970 an organization named the Institute of Underwater Research (IUR) in Dallas Texas initiated a thirty-day magnetometer survey of the Padre Island coastline. A combined twenty-four anomalies were recorded along twenty miles of coastline. Of the twenty-four anomalies that were recorded by the Dallas group, thirteen were investigated. The Arnold-Weddle volume is vague about this survey and its importance, as compared to what Platoro had accomplished with their initial remote sensing investigation. There was no information to be had on the Institute of Underwater Research, it was likely a cultural resource firm that specialized in remote sensing surveys for engineering firms and the oil industry.

Another magnetometer survey was made in 1972 by Carl Clausen and J. Barto Arnold that focused on the northernmost *San Esteban* site, the site that Platoro had surveyed during their magnetometer survey, but had not had time to excavate before they had been shut-down by state authorities. The excavation crew was comprised of Clausen and Arnold, the assistant archaeologist, along with three diver archaeological technicians, three students, and three locals. The team rigged up a prop-wash deflector rig that they artfully named an "ocean-bottom-sediment-displacement system". Arnold states that the first artifact and reference point they encountered was a large anchor along with a lead sounding weight and a silver disk, all in association with the ballast pile that protected what was left of the vessel's keel.

Several conglomerates were also recovered along with several more silver discs. Arnold wrote that bad weather hampered the first season's excavations. Rather than storms, the Texas team was hampered by the effect of prevailing southeast winds that led to the build-up of waves, often forcing the team off of the site by mid-afternoon. Although the artifact recovery count was not great, Arnold deemed the first season a success.

The State of Texas 1973 Field Season

The 1973 excavation began on June 30th. The investigation team was beefed up with students from the University of Texas and other academic institutions and the field investigation was operated as an archaeological field school. When field operations began the team consisted of fourteen students and a supervisory staff of eight. The Arnold-Weddle book confirmed the old mantra that students who were certified divers and had studied archaeology were preferred over students that needed diver certification. "The emphasis on archaeologists stemmed in part from our belief that it is preferable to make a diver out of an archaeologist than to make an archaeologist out of a diver."

The field methodology of the State of Texas 1973 field season was similar to the previous season. A barge was towed to the site and anchored. The barge could be re-positioned to excavate different sections of the site utilizing the blower by loosening and tightening the anchor ropes. The divers began to work the periphery of the wreck where they found an anchor. The ballast pile area and associated artifacts had been pinpointed through the magnetometer survey conducted in 1972. The artifacts recovered included a few scattered pieces of treasure... one silver disk and nine silver coins. Once the periphery of the shipwreck was inspected the divers used hand-held metal detectors to work into the wreck site. The divers found a home-made anchor on the site with an attached piece of line that they interpreted to be the nefarious evidence left behind by treasure hunters. The truth is that Platoro had been on the site, but had not had time for further investigate before being shut down by the State of Texas; the home-made anchor was evidence of a long-lost Platoro marker buoy.

As the overburden was removed from the ballast pile area the excavation revealed the presence of a portion of a ship's wooden keel and sternpost, about five meters in length, that had been preserved in the oxygen-free (anaerobic) sediments. The recovery of the ship's keel would prove to be one of the most important Padre Island discoveries and would serve to document the size of the *San Esteban*. It is impossible to know the depositional (erosion) history of the shipwreck site, however, the fact that a large portion of wood was preserved indicated that a good deal of drifted sand had covered the lower ship's hull in the days and months following the ship's sinking in 1554.

There were also large, heavy conglomerates on the site, groups of artifacts fused together, a process derived from iron objects lying in close proximity to one another and becoming chemically bonded. One explanation for the formation of the conglomerates is that the contents of shipping containers were trapped as a group by encrustation after the container had been crushed by shifting ballast, or that the artifacts were gathered together in depressions by chance currents, and there in close association became fused together by electrolytic bonding. These conglomerates were X-rayed and the findings were extraordinary: one conglomerate contained a broken verso (swivel gun), others, parts of an anchor, nails, and coins, along with pieces of iron rigging, and musket and cannonballs.

It was not all work and no play during the State of Texas investigation. Arnold writes that the student field school led to some modest partying by the student participants. The locus of evening activity was The Red Dog Saloon at Port Mansfield, and it seems that a good time was had by all. Billy related that the Platoro group was generally too tired after a hard day's work to engage in the local shrimper and commercial fisherman nightlife. Operating a small start-up salvage company and managing the excavation of the *Espiritu Santo* site was just about all that Billy could handle. Billy related that the shipwreck seemed to consume the time of all the serious salvage divers, there always seemed to be something to fix on the *Little Lady* and managing egos was an ongoing responsibility that had to be addressed on a daily basis!

Searching For a Salvage Camp

During the 1973 field season, the Texas Team conducted a four-day survey of the beach in the backshore area of the *San Esteban* and the *Espiritu Santo* sites. This area, that should have covered at least a mile, was believed to be the area where the castaways and salvage teams from Vera Cruz had set up temporary camps. Arnold reported that the primary artifact material discovered were ballast stones, thirty-one in total, along with other artifact material that included glass, encrusted iron, bone, and a sandstone abrader. Arnold believed that the only materials that could be definitely linked to the shipwrecks were the ballast stones; perhaps the iron objects were also shipwreck related, and the sandstone abrader may have been aboriginal. Arnold stated that some of the ballast stones were large and some small, and there seemed to be some clustering effect. Does it seem logical that castaways would collect ballast and bring it ashore? The only immediate uses of ballast stone would be to perhaps erect windbreaks, or to construct fire pits or a small fortification; the survey of the backshore area did not reveal any charcoal remains indicative of a fire. Since no excavation of the dunes was undertaken charcoal evidence would likely have been buried over the centuries through the natural wind-blown reconfiguration of the barrier island sand dunes.

Terrestrial excavation would likely have uncovered some additional evidence of earlier salvage activity. As the story goes, the 1554 survivors gathered on the shoreline following their shipwreck ordeal and accounts state that they began their trek south toward Mexico soon after being marooned. There is no doubt that the following, official and unofficial salvage efforts would have left considerable remains of short term habitation on the beach and there certainly had to be shore parties that worked from the beach as well as from vessels moored offshore. The beach opposite the shipwrecks is now part of a Federal National Seashore and metal detecting on the beaches is prohibited. A further sub-surface investigation for possible salvage camps on Padre Island is unlikely.

The Arnold-Weddle shipwreck history devotes a short paragraph to beach finds near the shipwreck sites. Beach finds were the bait that first brought the Znika brothers to Padre Island. Billy Kenon stated that most of the coin finds were retrieved from around the dredged entrance to Port Mansfield Channel the resting place of the *Santa Maria De Yciar*. When the channel was originally cut through the barrier island the coins were thrown up on shore in the sand spoil material deposited on the beach around the channel entrance. Billy believes that hundreds of 2 Real Carlos and Johanna coins have been recovered over the years, primarily by searchers with metal detectors. The best time to search was after heavy winds and rain incidents that washed away sand overburden exposing individual coins.

The Short 1975 Field Season

The investigators returned to Padre Island in the summer and fall of 1975. One important goal was to carry out a magnetometer survey of the area around the two known shipwreck sites as well as the area around the entrance to Port Mansfield Channel. Of special interest was the near-shore area between the shipwreck sites and the shoreline. Three anomalies were recorded in the vicinity of the middle wreck, the *Espiritu Santo*; upon examination, the largest anomaly turned out to be the scattered remains of a shrimp boat that had been lost in the surf zone, the second was part of an anchor, a ring and half of the anchor shank, along with six Carlos and Johanna coins. The third anomaly proved to be a water or fuel tank that was speculated to have been placed there by the treasure hunters to serve as a marker or point of reference used to relocate the site with a magnetometer after all the ferrous artifacts had been recovered from the site. Just north of the *San Esteban* site, the Texas investigators discovered another sixteenth-century anchor located south, and inshore of the wreck site. The investigators theorized that due to its position it was not a *San Esteban* anchor but an anchor from one of the small salvage vessels that was lost in the area, perhaps an anchor that was previously salvaged from one of the three shipwrecks.

As the State of Texas investigation was completed, it is necessary, to sum up the success of their investigation at Padre Island. At some cost to the citizens of Texas in tax dollars, it was ascertained, that the initial salvage operations after the 1554 shipwreck disaster, coupled with the Platoro salvage, had resulted in the recovery of most of the artifact material on the two shipwreck sites. Although the State of Texas investigations recovered a modest amount of artifact material, as well as the important recovery of the *San Esteban* keel, the Texas State investigations may be considered successful but expensive. The bottom line was that Platoro had recovered most of the artifact material and treasure, and also performed a competent artifact conservation program as overseen by Mendel Peterson the Director of Underwater Exploration for the Smithsonian Institution.

What Did It Cost

The Arnold-Weddle book documents the cost of the State of Texas Padre Island investigation; this cost information bears examination. All of the monies were appropriated from the State of Texas Revenues through The Texas Antiquities Committee. There were five categories of project expenditures; these included (a) Fieldwork (b) Texas Historical Commission funds; (c) Artifact conservation costs; (d) Document Research and Translation costs; and (e) Museum Exhibit costs. The fieldwork expenditure was $250,000; the Texas Historical Commission pitched in an additional $30,000 for fieldwork as well. Conservation costs were attributed at $97,000; it is not clear if Texas had to re-cycle some of the Platoro artifacts that had been conserved at the Platoro conservation facility in Indiana. While Doris Olds in *Texas Legacy from the Gulf* criticizes Platoro for some methodological shortcomings, that they were performing when they were shut down, she did not voice any criticism of the extensive Platoro conservation efforts that were overseen by Mendel Peterson of the Smithsonian Institution. Additionally, some $54,000 was spent on document research and translation, and $40,000 for museum exhibits. The total expenditures for the State of Texas was a reported $471,000. There is no entry for the 1975 remote sensing survey that was likely a $50, 000 dollar expenditure. All told, eliminating the 1975 remote sensing expenditure, the cost for the State of Texas archaeological salvage was $471,000, or with the remote sensing survey round the cost off to $500,000. In today's dollars, a 1975 half-million dollar investment would probably compute to 1.5 million dollars. Billy Kenon believes that the short Platoro season of 1967 and the months spent before the season kicked off had cost Platoro in the area of a quarter-million dollars. The monies spent by the project hangers-on and peripheral costs are unknown. The cost of the litigation on the part of the State of Texas and Platoro is another issue and difficult to compute accurately. The money wasted in court by both the State of Texas and Platoro, and the additional money spent by Billy Kenon litigating on his own against the state might have been better spent if Platoro and the Texas authorities could have entered into some workable partnership as had been the case in Florida.

Billy Meets Carl Clausen

One interesting and puzzling sentence in the Arnold and Weddle *Nautical Archaeology of Padre Island* volume is found on page 191 and reads: "Unfortunately the site plans with the locations of all artifacts recovered in 1972 and 1973 have disappeared from our agency files, as have the original field notes containing the measurements and provenience data necessary for reconstructing the site plan." What happened to these important archaeological documents that included the precise measurements of artifact associations and other site plan data? The question posed is straightforward and very important. How did the site plans disappear from the safe-keeping of the Texas Antiquities Committee? Did an insider, perhaps an archaeologist or a trusted student borrow the site plans and then fail to return them to the project headquarters, or did someone try to sabotage the project by destroying the plans — who knows? Also, why did Clausen leave his Texas Antiquities Committee position? Was he truly tired of administering acrimonious treasure salvage programs, or was there another issue, or a personal vendetta that ended Clausen's short sojourn to the Lone Star State?

Following his departure from Texas, Clausen drifted into the

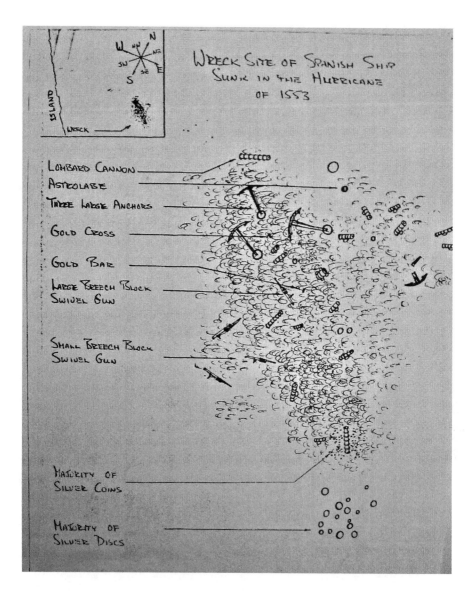

Mysteriously, the site plan for the Esperitu Santo has disappeared from the official Texas archives. Fortunately, Billy Kenon maintained a hand-drawn copy in his own records as seen above. Illustration: Billy Kenon

Opposite page: a 3D reconstruction of the artifacts as found on the Espiratu Santo site. Illustration: T. L. Armstrong

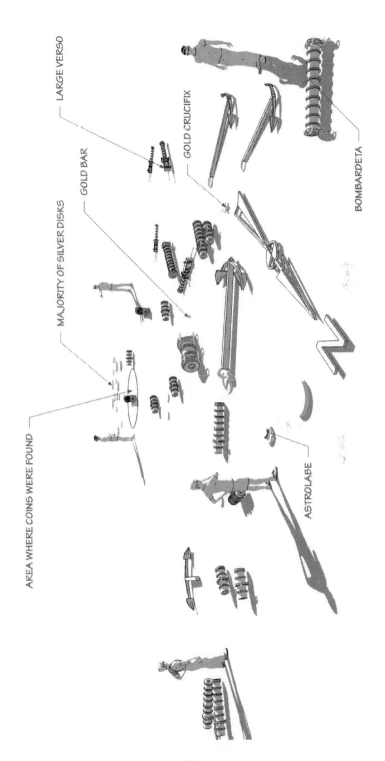

world of professional archaeology, or 'compliance archaeology' as the specialization is often called. Clausen stayed busy with short-term contract archaeology projects that consisted of remote sensing surveys associated with beach re-nourishment, and other public works projects that paid a decent wage but did not offer the excitement and challenge of shipwreck archaeology. Clausen also drifted into what might be considered para-military security work that would eventually lead to a new career in rural Florida as a law enforcement officer. People who knew Clausen well remarked on his interest in firearms, and what would today be considered survivalist skills. Clausen and his wife Cynthia lived in a double-wide mobile home on fifty acres of woodland not too far from the Florida capitol in Tallahassee.

On July 22, 1997, something went wrong in the Clausen rural home in Sycamore, Florida. By all accounts Carl and Cynthia Clausen had a troubled marriage; both drank to excess and fought constantly. Cynthia worked as a social worker at the nearby state mental hospital in Chattahoochee, and Carl Clausen had most recently been a police officer in the small town of Midway, Florida. Carl had recently been bypassed for the job of Police Chief in Midway, and in frustration had resigned. To add psychological insult to injury, Clausen had recently discovered that Cynthia had re-kindled a relationship with an old boyfriend via the internet. It seems that the failure to achieve the police chief position, linked to the internet issue, fueled by alcohol abuse pushed Clausen over the edge

Reports vary, but the sad story is that on the afternoon or evening of July 22, 1997, Clausen and his wife became involved in an altercation that led to Clausen shooting and killing his wife, along with the family dog that was beloved to them both. After the shooting, Clausen, armed with handguns and a semi-automatic assault rifle, and attired in camouflage gear, fled into the sanctuary of the dense north Florida woods. Shortly after the murder of Cynthia Clausen was discovered, the local police erected a number of roadblocks at strategic area cross-roads. Approaching one roadblock on foot, Clausen opened fire with his assault rifle seriously wounding one police officer and less seriously two others. To make a long story short, after five days of hunkering down in the woods, Clausen, cold, tired and hungry, returned to his trailer in the woods where his ex-son-in-law, a Tallahassee police detective, surprised Clausen and took him into custody. Several days previously the police had withdrawn the roadblocks in a ruse to draw Clausen in — it worked!

At Clausen's trial, he pled guilty and was sentenced to fifty years in prison. Today Clausen languishes in the Florida State penitentiary system. At the time of the murder in 1997, Clausen was 60 years old; today in 2019 Clausen would be close to 81 years old. What happened to Carl Clausen as an archaeologist, as a late-career law enforcement officer, and then as some have described him, a Soldier of Fortune?

In interviews for this book, Billy Kenon was asked if he had ever encountered Carl Clausen after Platoro had been shut down, and Clausen had assumed the position of State of Texas Underwater Archaeologist. Billy replied in the negative that he never encountered Clausen until he (Billy) attended a shipwreck conference in Fort Lauderdale, Florida in 1985. This was more than a decade after Clausen had departed the State of Texas Antiquities Commission, and Billy was still fighting the battle to sue the State of Texas.

The 1985 Fort Lauderdale Shipwreck Symposium was held at a Lauderdale, beachfront hotel. This was one of a number of conference — cum workshop attempts to bring archaeologists, treasure hunters, and sports divers together to discuss their differences and find some sort of common ground of cooperation. This was not the first attempt to bring archaeologists and treasure hunters into some sort of truce, where the acrimonious bickering and bad blood between the ivory tower archaeologists and treasure hunters could be tempered by logic and good sense. The Fort Lauderdale conference was a mixed bag of notorious treasure hunters like Bob Marx, and Mel Fisher, along with archaeologists Peter Throckmorton, Duncan Mathewson and a handful of cultural resource protection advocates from state agencies and universities the most prominent being Sonny Cockrell from the Florida Division of Historical Resources. According to Billy not much happened at the symposium, other than some obligatory workshops where the "non-renewable resource vs treasure as profit mavens" argued and pontificated. Peripheral to the symposium was a magnetometer survey for a legendary Nazi submarine believed to be lost off Fort Lauderdale, at the edge of the Gulf Stream. This submarine hunt diversion came up empty, and most participants found comradeship and diversion at the hotel bar.

It was in this environment that an acquaintance pointed out to Billy, that the former State of Texas Underwater Archaeologist, Carl Clausen, was standing at the end of the hotel bar having a beverage. Billy took note of Clausen who was talking with a couple of young sun-tanned guys that could have been treasure divers or archaeology graduate students — Billy didn't know. Taking an aw shucks attitude, Billy approached Clausen, said "excuse me" and introduced himself. At first, Clausen did not seem to recognize the name, then Billy said, "Platoro" and "Padre Island"; this got Clausen's attention! The two young divers quickly excused themselves and departed the scene. As Billy remembers, he and Clausen chatted for ten or fifteen minutes; the conservation was neither overly friendly nor acrimonious. Today, Billy remembers little of what was said!

Later that same day Billy was leaving the hotel when he was approached by one of the young men that had been standing with Clausen at the bar. Billy remembers that some of the treasure hunter participants were openly buying and trading coins; this was neither illegal nor unethical. Treasure hunters deal in coins all the time at coin shows, or in any venue they so choose. If an archaeologist dealt in coins their peers would judge this behavior as unethical. Ethics was, of course, one of the themes of the Shipwreck Symposium; could any common ground be found between the treasure hunters and archaeologists? To continue the story, the young man that approached Billy asked him if he would like to "look at some Padre Island coins." Surprised and intrigued Billy said, "sure!" It had been a long time since Billy had seen or handled a Carlos and Johanna coin. The coins were in an envelope and Billy counted ten nicely conserved, high-grade coins. "How much ?" Billy asked. "Hundred apiece." countered the young man. Billy said nothing, quickly examined the coins, reached for his wallet, removed ten, one hundred dollar bills, and exchanged them for the coins. They thanked one another and Billy never saw the young coin dealer, or Carl Clausen again.

It seems strange that someone who had discovered a treasure trove of shipwreck artifacts, would at any point, have to purchase coins on the open market, that for every logical reason they should own. In Florida the agreement between the state and the treasure hunters was simple and straightforward; the state received twenty percent of the overall treasure and all one-of-a-kind artifacts. Thus at Padre Island, the State of Texas would have taken twenty percent of the coins and the one-of-a-kind artifacts like the tiny gold cross and perhaps one of the most historically important astrolabes, and crossbow. As we have seen the state took all of the artifacts and gave Platoro what amounted to a buy out. As a matter of fact, in Florida, the rare coins, those that were of special numismatic value went into a state study collection that was open to inspection by scholars and anyone with a serious interest in numismatics. The treasure hunters could do anything they wanted with their coins, sell them to friends and associates, auction houses, or have them made into jewelry that would enhance their marketability.

One of the problems that Florida had foreseen in their treasure program was the possibility of coin theft by the treasure hunters. During the Clausen era in Florida, the state had initiated a program where state agents were placed onboard all of the licensed and approved salvage vessels. The agent's job was to monitor the activities onboard the salvage vessels, and of course, make sure that all the state regulations were followed. Terry Armstrong has documented the utilization of state agents in his book *The Rainbow Chasers*. In that book Armstrong points out that that the agents performed several functions; monitoring the behavior of the treasure hunters, to make sure that there was no pilfering of artifacts and treasure, and also by logging the recoveries and excavations of the salvors using sextants against landmarks on shore.

One of the by-products of the Florida treasure salvage program and the division of artifacts and treasure between the state and the treasure hunters has been the production of books and monographs that document the importance of the artifact collection. In Florida two important books have evolved from the salvage program, both dealing with the numismatics of the gold and silver coin collections. A numismatist, Dr. Alan Craig, a professor at Florida Atlantic University has produced two important and definitive books describing the State of Florida coin collections, these are titled, *Spanish Colonial Silver Coins in the Florida Collection'* and *Spanish Colonial Gold Coins in the Florida Collection*; neither of these books would have been produced without the Florida treasure salvage program.

It also appears that Platoro's, Znika brothers, both experienced beach metal detector buffs, had to go on the open market (like Billy) to purchase a sample of the coins that they were responsible for recovering from the shipwreck. Even before the discovery of the shipwreck site, the brothers had beach find specimens of coins that likely came from the wreck at the mouth of Port Mansfield Channel. While going through Billy Kenon's copious treasure trove records, I found a letter that had been written from a coin dealer to Paul Znika; it is unknown if this communication was just a query or if Paul Znika actually purchased coins from International Coins and Currency of Montpelier, Vermont. The letter refers to the "First silver coins of the Americas", and goes on to document the provenance of the coins, "a treasure cache found in Mexico City." These coins were likely non-shipwreck coins, a simple test could ascertain if they were! What is important about this letter, other than Znika might have wanted shipwreck era coins, is that International Coins price for a Carlos and Johanna coin was $128.00, which depending on the condition seems fair. We have to remember that Platoro felt that Mendel Peterson's valuation for the coins was a little low. As a matter of fact, Peterson had been aided in his evaluation by Frank Sedwick a very experienced Florida numismatist. It seems that Billy's purchase of 'pretty good' specimens of coins that likely came from Padre Island was a bargain.

Artifact Conservation in Texas

On September 24, 1969, Texas Court Judge Paul Martineau had ordered that the Platoro Group artifacts be placed in the temporary custody of TARL, the Texas Archaeological Research Laboratory at Balcones Research center on the University of Texas campus at Austin, where a conservation laboratory was constructed expressly for the shipwreck artifacts. On October 14, 1969 part of the collection, consisting mainly of gold and silver was delivered to the lab; precious metals were placed in a vault, ferrous unstable items were immersed in tanks, and containers and stable items like ballast stones placed on shelves in a storage area. An interesting bit of information was that, what was labeled "a small separate collection" was delivered to TARL in

March 1972. This artifact material had been recovered by the Institute for Underwater Research (IUR) a non-profit affiliated with Southern Methodist University in Dallas, Texas. IUR had been contracted to carry out a comprehensive remote sensing survey of the sites, but apparently had also been engaged in artifact recovery.

In her book *Texas Legacy From The Gulf*, Doris Olds states that when the artifacts were confiscated from Platoro by the authorities and delivered to the laboratory, there was no precise information on their provenience — their wreck of origin. This confirms the hostility and lack of communication that existed between the Platoro Group and the authorities. At the time that Platoro was enjoined from working the site, the artifacts excavated had originated on the middle site, the *Espiritu Santo*, and only a cursory survey of the northernmost wreck, the *San Esteban* had been conducted, with only a few artifact recoveries. We should remember that when the injunction barring Platoro from working in the field was invoked and when Platoro was ordered to turn over the artifacts to the state the treasure hunters had also turned in a large amount of wreck associated paper-work along with the artifacts and had never seen the paperwork again. Perhaps the Platoro paperwork disappeared with the other site plans prepared during the two seasons the Clausen-Arnold team spent in the field.

In her introduction to the *Texas Legacy From The Gulf* book, sub-titled, *History of Recovery and Delivery to TARL* Doris Olds offers her opinion on the artifact collection as related to the collection's ability to speak to illuminate the archaeology of Padre Island. Olds writes "Because the Platoro group's goal was the recovery of treasure, the range of materials probably is biased in favor of what might prove to be monetarily valuable." Olds continues, "Apparently little or no effort was made to map the site or record information that would preserve the orientation, association, or location of the various objects before they were disturbed. Hence, much priceless information has been lost forever, reducing the historic and scientific value of this distinctive assemblage." Olds concludes this rant with a final emotional observation, "With only a few pages of Platoro's dive records accompanying the collection, there is no certainty of the number of wrecks actually involved in its operations."

Again, this is not accurate. The Platoro Group had mapped

the *Espiritu Santo* site and when the artifact assemblage was confiscated the important site plan notes with individual artifact sheets were turned over to Commissioner Sadler, and as far as Billy Kenon knows the artifacts went directly to TARL. Remember that Mendel Peterson, the Platoro archaeologist, had assumed oversight of the Platoro collection, and regularly traveled from Washington D.C. to Gary, Indiana to supervise the artifact stabilization and conservation process. Although Platoro dragged their feet in returning the artifacts to the Texas authorities, it should also be remembered that the Platoro Group salvage moved along quickly under the direction of Billy Kenon, and the dive team. It would have made better sense for the Texas authorities to approach Platoro, and perhaps try to find some common ground where the treasure hunters and the state could work together. Barto Arnold and the Texas Antiquities Commission had to virtually start from scratch with their separate investigation, which in three seasons, found significantly less treasure and artifact material than Platoro had in one season.

Leave No Stone Unturned

Another interesting story emerged as this book neared completion. In a National Park Service publication describing the establishment of the Padre Island National Seashore in September 1962, another version of the shipwreck discovery was published. The NPS article confirms the many coin discoveries on the beach in the area of the Port Mansfield Channel, but the article states that "the finds amounted to very little." How the park service knew the amount of coins discovered over the years is not elaborated upon; certainly they did not want to encourage coin prospecting on the Padre Island beaches. The article also relates that in 1964 a woman named Vida Lee Connor was on a scuba diving adventure off of Padre Island and "discovered the location of the shipwrecks." The article goes on to say that Ms. Connor conducted two years of research, published a pamphlet about her discovery, and marked the site with buoys. The pamphlet was entitled *Ancient Galleon Sails Again and Treasures Recovered off of Padre Island*. As the story goes, Connor returned later and discovered that the site was being excavated; this must have been the Platoro Group working the site in 1967. This NPS article goes on to describe the Platoro excavation of the *Espiritu Santo* site and the intervention by the State of Texas, along with the ensuing legal battle over the shipwreck site. The article also states that in 1974, the three shipwreck sites were listed on the National Register of Historic Places and this led to the establishment of the area as the Mansfield Cut Underwater Archaeological District. We were unable to locate the Vida Lee Connor pamphlet describing her adventures. It is interesting that the NPS would include this information when it was well known that the *Espiritu Santo* site was buried in many feet of sediment; both Platoro and the later Barto Arnold excavations had to excavate this overburden to expose the site. The Connor story is intriguing. What did she actually find offshore Padre Island in 1964?

Museum Treasure

After all the artifacts and treasure were transferred from the Platoro conservation facility to the State of Texas conservation laboratory in Austin, the state officials began to plan for an exhibition of the Padre Island shipwreck artifact collection. As conceived by the state cultural authorities there would be permanent exhibits as well as small traveling exhibits that could be shown in local venues, and then move on from one site to another.

Treasure museums fit into a unique sphere of the discipline known as museology, the art and craft of presenting any cultural assemblage as an exhibition. Of course with the announcement that there would be a museum exhibit, there was the obligatory smear campaign by the Texas Archaeological Research Facility (TARL). Of course the criticism in Doris Olds, *Texas Legacy From The Sea* was of a generic nature; the Platoro operation was just "treasure hunters" and TARL at the University of Texas, Austin, were the true professionals. But there were no real substantive criticisms of the Platoro conservation of artifacts efforts. After all, the State of Texas had to travel to Indiana to the Platoro conservation laboratory to retrieve the artifacts, and that in and of itself was not conducive to stabilizing the artifact assemblage. Many of the artifacts were fused together in conglomerates, and this called for the X-ray of these concreted clumps of material to ascertain what was inside the rock-like clumps of fused cultural material. Once TARL X-rayed the conglomerates in Austin, then a conservation strategy could be followed that would allow the freeing of artifacts so additional conservation could be undertaken.

Treasure museums had been established since the days of the Real Eight Corporation and the Mel Fisher Treasure Salvors Corporation in the 1960s and 1970s. Mel Fisher established state of the art museums in Key West and Sebastian, Florida that were associated with the 1715 Treasure Coast shipwrecks and the 1622 fleet disaster that had a focus on the riches of the *Atocha* and *Santa Margarita* shipwrecks. Fisher's Sebastian venue offered a retrospective of the 1715 artifacts and a conservation laboratory that was visible from the museum display area where tourists could watch the conservators as they processed artifacts as they were brought from field sites to the museum facility. In Key West, the Fisher headquarters offered the same fare of treasure and artifacts as well as a strong-room where the silver bars of the *Atocha* mother lode were stacked up like railroad ties... a truly spectacular exhibit.

Treasure is difficult to display, this is especially true of coins and gold bars that in the best of times are difficult to protect, and after a quick display of these artifacts, the museum visitor is ready to move on to more substantive exhibits where artifacts like firearms and the every-day tools and kitchenware that were used by passengers and crew were showcased. At the Fisher museum, the gold and silver artifacts were largely reproductions but were reproductions that were difficult to differentiate from real coins and gold bars. At the Fisher museum in Key West, an authentic gold bar had been placed in a small display case where the museum visitor could reach in and heft the bar but could not remove it. One clever thief using a heavy-duty tool cut away a portion of the display case and made off with the gold bar. That was the end of that exhibit!

The State of Florida also sponsored two museum venues, one in the state capitol in Tallahassee and the other directly on the beach near Sebastian Inlet. The Sebastian Inlet museum venue was not as flashy as the two Fisher venues, and tended to present exhibits with a focus on educational exhibits like the 1715 salvage camp that was only about 100 feet north of the museum in a paved-over area of the parking lot. The Sebastian venue is also directly on the beach where the museum visitors could walk out of the rear entrance of the museum and view the beach and surf much like the survivors of the 1715 fleet disaster had experienced the natural environment at the time of their shipwreck. The treasure exhibits sponsored by the State of Florida was a pioneer effort to regulate archaeological salvage; unpopular in the wider archaeological community the Florida treasure salvage program essentially became a win-win proposition.

In Texas, since the state was clearly in the driver's seat, the museum venues and exhibits were all the responsibility of the state. Billy kept all the newspaper and magazine accounts of the museum exhibits and museum openings. In a September 1980, "South Padre Island Parade" article the exhibit at the McAllen International Museum is showcased. The exhibit is well done, with an emphasis on history rather than treasure. A large anchor is exhibited in the center of the venue with wall displays of astrolabes, a cannon, a crossbow and an assemblage of Carlos and Johanna silver coins. Also included are the less exotic artifacts that include hull nails, spikes, and wood fragments. The exhibit is titled, "Treasure, People, Ships and Dreams". The Texas Antiquities Committee is cited as the sponsor of the exhibit, but in a gesture to Platoro, Martha McClain the journalist who wrote the story writes that "Operating under the name of Plataro Ltd, and an independent firm headed by Billy Kenon of Laguna Vista, found the galleon wreckage two weeks before Hurricane Beulah struck the South Texas coast". At the time of the exhibit in 1980, the Platoro-Kenon lawsuit was still being heard by the U.S. Fifth Circuit Court of Appeals.

The traveling treasure exhibits visited a large number of Texas towns and cities that included Dallas, San Antonio, Corpus Christi, Lubbock, El Paso, Huston, Fort Worth, Austin, McAllen, and Canyon. The exhibit venues were both mobile and fixed and ran for varying amounts of time. The exhibits were both anthropological as well as archaeological in nature, having a strong emphasis on the Spanish seafarers, their tools, weapons, and lives aboard ship. Exhibits also featured the conservation and preservation of the artifacts and the work of conservator Dr. Donny Hamilton the TARL expert who had received the assemblage of artifacts from the Platoro conservation facility as transferred from Gary, Indiana.

One popular exhibit was a large encrusted conglomerate a crusty artifact that was, at best puzzling, until a large X-ray next to the blackened clump revealed the treasure within. Eventually freed from the confines of the conglomerates which weighed as much as 300 pounds were artifacts as diverse as portions of cannon barrels, bits of wood, rope, pewter tableware, silver coins and even pieces of food and a few stray cockroaches. Utilizing the X-rays as an artifact roadmap the TARL conservators were able to use small pneumatic drills to free select artifacts so that they could be further conserved through electrolytic reversal and other sensitive means of preservation. Some artifacts encased within the conglomerates had completed deteriorated. These ghost-like objects were rescued and preserved by casts being made of the impressions.

Billy tells of his visiting the exhibit when it toured his old home town of Raymondville, Texas. Raymondville was Billy's first home when, as an adolescent, his family moved from Florida to Texas. Billy is generally quiet about the exhibit; it undoubtedly must be a strange experience to enter an exhibition and look at artifacts and treasure that you recovered, but never really had a chance to examine in a conserved state, where the beauty and importance of the assemblage was made most manifest. The fact that Billy and his team recovered most of the artifacts that were displayed, undoubtedly gave him pride and satisfaction of a job well done.

Hindsight is 20/20

The saga of the Padre Island Shipwrecks lasted more than twenty years before there was a settlement that, in truth, was never acceptable to Billy Kenon. In the mind of Billy, the shipwrecks are an ever-present memory that he carries with him every day. The fact that the Platoro Group had broken no laws when they went into the field off of Padre Island is of little consolation when faced with the fact that the government had confiscated the entire artifact assemblage, leaving Platoro with a pat on the back, a few dollars in settlement, and ludicrous permission to make copies of a few artifacts. Billy maintains to this day that Platoro endeavored to do the right thing, by retaining a competent archaeologist, Mendel Peterson, and initially conserving and safe-keeping the important assemblage of shipwreck artifacts.

No doubt the Texas Archaeological Research Lab (TARL) had a larger budget and larger staff to conserve, preserve, and then exhibit the shipwreck artifacts in a museum setting. The fact is, Platoro took the initiative and risk by going into the field to recover a shipwreck that might never have been recovered given the attitude of the State of Texas historic preservation lobby. It's easy to place blame; remember, the site plans that had been prepared by Arnold and Clausen disappeared from the files, as did the site plan that had been prepared by Kenon and his underwater recovery team. The *Espiritu Santo* site plan that has been published in this book is a reconstruction prepared to utilize the notes and diagrams so carefully preserved by Kenon in his private files. It should also be remembered that when the Port Mansfield ship channel was dredged through Padre Island in 1957 by the Army Corps of Engineers, it is believed that the historic remains of the *Santa Maria de Yciar* were obliterated, and the beach around the entrance to the channel became a treasure trove for metal detectorists. No one, especially this author, can blame the government for this destruction; in the 1950s there was no requirement that a cultural resource archaeological assessment and a magnetometer survey be performed pursuant to the dredging project. This period, the first few decades after World War II was the dawn of shipwreck archaeology. There was no real knowledge of the extent of the historic shipwreck resources that lay undiscovered in the coastal waters of the United States. Florida undoubtedly had the richest of these historic shipwrecks, containing the remains of three Spanish fleets, those of 1622, 1715 and 1733, and that the waters off the Texas coast were also the site of important colonial period shipwrecks.

Another fallacy of the shipwreck preservation lobby holds that shipwrecks are time capsules and should be left undisturbed until some (illusory) date in the future when archaeological science can excavate shipwrecks in a technically more efficient manner. This is preservationist propaganda. The truth is that shipwrecks left undisturbed, whether buried in sediment or exposed to the energy of the tide and current deteriorate at various rates. It is true that shipwrecks that might be buried very quickly in an oxygen-free environment tend to have a higher rate of preservation than those exposed to the natural oxygen-infused environment. Remember, shipwrecks exposed to the elements in the tropics will be consumed by shipworms, and the action of salt working on iron and silver coins will trigger a high rate of deterioration. Case in point, many of the artifacts that were discovered in conglomerate forms, and conserved by TARL were found to be deteriorated to varying degrees; iron cannon like the versos and lombards (bombardettas) are also susceptible to deterioration and must spend many months, if not years, in the electrolytic reversal process to be preserved. The two classifications of artifacts that do not deteriorate at a rapid rate are gold and bronze. This ratio of artifact deterioration in the natural environment begs for archaeological recovery, conservation, preservation, curation, and eventually display in a cultural setting — a museum.

To this point, it seems ludicrous that Mendel Peterson, of the Smithsonian Institution, who was routinely visiting the Platoro conservation facility in Indiana would have associated himself with a slip-shod organization that was mishandling the 1554 artifact assemblage. Since Platoro was shut down after a short period in the field, there was insufficient time for Peterson to take the project generated information and prepare acceptable archaeological reports. It seems that the information in the Platoro laboratory was also turned over to the State of Texas when the artifacts were transferred to Austin. Peterson was a well-known and respected maritime historian, who at the dawn of the new sub-discipline of underwater archaeology would never have violated the standards of the day. The basic question here would be: why would Mendel Peterson jeopardize his standing in the archaeological community, and his position at the Smithsonian, by doing a sub-standard job at Padre Island? No doubt, Peterson, caught off guard by the intervention by the State of Texas, and the collapse of the Platoro Group just had to walk away from the project. It would have been interesting if Platoro had received the contract that had been promised by Commissioner Jerry Sadler, and Peterson was eventually able to write a popular history of the *Espiritu Santo* and *San Esteban* shipwrecks.

Billy's quest to gain some sort of recognition for the Platoro team has spanned the decades from the mid-1960s to the writing of this book in the second decade of the twenty-first century, a period of over fifty years. Billy was a young man when he went into the field with the Platoro Group, and is now (2019) 77 years old. Many of the Platoro team are now deceased. Without Billy sponsoring the writing of this book, the Platoro side of the Padre Island Shipwreck story would never have been told. Clearly, the objective of this book has been to offer a more balanced account of the story, while not taking away from the strictly archaeological account of the shipwreck recovery as documented in the Arnold and Weddle, *Nautical Archaeology of Padre Island* account of the shipwrecks. It is, however, safe to say that without the work of Billy Kenon and the Platoro Group, that two important shipwrecks, the *Espiritu Santo* and the *San Esteban* might never have been recovered leaving us without the benefit of an important chapter in American Maritime History.

Billy Kenon, 2019
Photo: Robert H. Baer

The Artifact Assemblage

Coins

The Padre Island shipwrecks produced a disappointing number of coins, an indication of thorough salvage in the aftermath of the 1554 shipwreck disaster, and perhaps by other salvage operations in years after. The definitive compilation of how many artifacts and the category of the recovered artifacts are recorded in the inventory found in *The Nautical Archaeology of Padre Island*. A compilation is made of the coins recovered by Platoro and by the Texas Historical Commission during the salvage years, in 1967, 1972, 1973, and 1975.

The State of Texas Archaeologists recovered a total of 362 coins over three short field seasons. The coins are in the following category and numbers, 1-Real, silver, Carlos and Johanna. Mexico City Mint (1); 2-Real silver, Carlos and Johanna. Mexico City Mint (114); 4-Real, silver, Carlos and Johanna, Mexico City Mint (209); Four other coins were recovered, one copper coin from the Santo Domingo Mint and two 4-Real, Carlos and Johanna, F assayer coins. An additional 1-Real, silver, Ferdinand and Isabella, Seville Mint coin was recovered. There were also 34 fragmentary coins so worn that the numismatics could not be made out.

When the State of Texas General Land Commission confiscated the Platoro collection of coins the overall count was 1,292 coins. The largest category of coins, 693 specimens were listed as, 4-Real Carlos and Johanna, Mexico City Mint, late series; of the 693 specimens, only 516 were categorized, as whole and in good condition; the second category by number of recovered coins numbered 136 coins, 2-Real Carlos and Johanna, Mexico City Mint late series; of the 136 coins recovered only 111 coins were categorized as whole and in good condition. All of the remaining coins were in poor, fragmentary, sulphided or completely disintegrated condition leaving only hollow molds formed by encrustation.

All of the identifiable coins, both silver and the few copper coins are referred to by coin experts as Carlos and Johanna coinage and as the breakdown of the assemblage shows all of the recovered shipwreck coins, except for one specimen from the Santo Domingo Mint. The first mint in the New World was the Mexico City mint founded in the reign of Charles I of Spain in 1536. Charles is an Anglicization of Carlos and his mother was Johanna, the daughter of Ferdinand and Isabella the Spanish monarchs that dispatched Christopher Columbus on his voyage of discovery in 1492. Johanna was considered mentally disturbed and was confined to a convent until her death in 1555. Charles reigned until his death in 1556.

The Padre Island coin assemblage is important for both historical and numismatic reasons. Since the conquest of the Aztecs by Cortez, the gold confiscated by the Spanish had generally been melted down into planchets or splashes and shipped in that form to Spain until the Mexico City mint was established in 1536.

The best way and sometimes the only way to identify a historic shipwreck was by the dates on coins, and from mint marks and assayer marks on bullion bars that can be referenced to a ship's manifest. The lack of dates on the Charles and Johanna coins as well as armory marks on bronze cannons that can be matched to a manifest was another limiting factor in identifying the shipwrecks. The numismatist Alan Craig in his *Spanish Colonial Silver Coins in the Florida Collection* sums up the dating void writing, "Collectors of Mexican Cob coinage have been accustomed to long and often disappointing searches for dated specimens." Craig offers a simple reason for the lack of dates due to a problem in the design of the coins; Craig writes, "The single date of the Mexican design, located only on the legend near the rim, was unlikely to be preserved in the normal course of Mexico minting practices. Since planchets were anything but round, chances were not good all four digits would be struck where they could be seen."

Silver Coin Summation

There are several ways to explain the small number of coins salvaged on the Padre Island shipwreck sites. The first is, of course, the immediate salvage of the vessels in the wake of the shipwreck event. The rapid response by the locals from Panuco and Vera Cruz resulted in a substantial recovery of coins and bullion in the weeks following the shipwreck. The slower Spanish bureaucratic response resulted in a slower, more methodical salvage of the three shipwrecks. In the following years, there were more forays to the site and the wreckage undoubtedly yielded more coins and treasure over the decade following the shipwrecks. There was probably little or no attempt by the coastal Indians to pillage the shipwreck sites; however, they were likely beachcombing for many months afterward for cargo that had buoyancy and floated ashore. The immediate Spanish salvage efforts recovered most of the easily assessable treasure. After the discovery of the wreck sites by Platoro the two wrecks north of Mansfield Cut the *Espiritu Santo* and the *San Esteban* were investigated and salvaged, respectively by Platoro and the Texas Antiquities Commission.

Billy Kenon believes that there is substantially more treasure located near the entrance to Port Mansfield channel. This may have been substantiated by a remote sensing survey that was done in February 1990 by an ocean engineering firm for the U.S. Army Corps of Engineers headquartered at Galveston, Texas. The report substantiates Billy Kenon's belief that portions of the Santa Maria exist in the shallows off the channel entrance. The report states that "A high probability exists that a portion of this wreck remains on the seafloor at the location of Anomaly Cluster A in the immediate vicinity of the Port Mansfield entrance channel. The presence of several smaller anomaly clusters west of Anomaly Cluster A suggests the possibility that wreckage from this vessel also lies scattered landward of the main wreck site within, or in close proximity to, the channel and a large anomaly located seaward of Anomaly Cluster A may be caused by an anchor from the *Santa Maria de Yciar*."

Two 4 reales from the Padre Island wrecks. Courtesy of Dan Sedwick LLC.

Artifact List per Platoro

This is a comprehensive list of all of the artifact material that was recovered by the Platoro Group and over a period of time and transferred to the State of Texas artifact deposit – TARL – Texas Archaeological Research Laboratory at the University of Texas, Austin. The vessel has been tentatively identified as the *Espiritu Santo* – 41WY3.
Total Objects in artifact assemblage 2,994

1. Coins, Two-real Carlos and Johanna Coins, Mexico City - Late Series (Total 136)
(1) Whole, good condition (111)
(2) Whole, poor condition (2)
(3) Fragmentary, good condition (14)
(4) Fragmentary, poor condition (9)

2. Probable 2-real Carlos and Johanna Coins, Mexico City Mint (Total 2)

3. 2-real Carlos and Johanna Coins, Mexico City Mint – Early Series (Total 11)
(1) Whole good condition (6)
(2) Whole, poor condition (1)
(3) Fragmentary, good condition (1)
(4) Fragmentary, poor conditions (2)

4. 2-real Carlos and Johanna Coin – Series Unknown (Total 1)
Partially encrusted – display as is. (1)

5. 3-real Carlos and Johanna Coin, Mexico City Mint – Early Series (Total 1)
(1) Whole, good condition (1)

6. 4-real Carlos and Johanna Coins, Mexico City Mint – Late Series
(Total 693)
(1) Whole, good condition (516)
(2) Whole, poor condition (69)
(3) Fragmentary, good condition (12)
(4) Fragmentary, poor condition (95)
(5) Whole, good condition, encrusted, for display (1)

7. Probable 4-real Carlos and Johanna Coins, Mexico City Mint – Late Series
(1) Poor, fragmentary (12)

8. 4-real Carlos and Johanna, Mexico City Mint – Early Series
(1) Whole, good condition (8)
(2) Fragmentary, good condition (1)

9. 4-real Carlos and Johanna Coins – Series Unknown
(1) Fragmentary, poor condition (1)

10. Probable 4-real Carlos and Johanna Coins – Series Unknown
(1) Fragmentary, poor condition (1)

11. 4-real Carlos and Johanna Coin, Santo Domingo Mint
(1) Whole, good condition (1)

12. Unidentified Carlos and Johanna Coins – Late Series
(1) Fragmentary, poor condition (1)

13. Probable Carlos and Johanna Coins – Denomination and Series Unknown
(1) Fragmentary, poor condition (9)

14. 4-maravedes Copper Coins
(1) Whole, good condition (1)
(2) Whole, poor condition (3)
(3) Fragmentary, poor condition (1)

15. Disintegrated Silver Coins, Converted to Sulphide (Total 231)
Left encrusted, x-ray showed little, loose coins, and encrusted

16. Molds of Coins Formed by Encrustation
Chemical break-down (231)

17. Silver Disks (ingots) (Total 53)
(1) Large (5)
(2) Medium (3)
(3) Small (11)
(4) Fragments (2)

18. Probable Silver thimble (Total 1)
Badly corroded

19. Gold objects (Total 2)
(1) Small crucifix (1)
(2) Ingot (1)

20. Cannons, Wrought Iron (Total 8)
(1) Swivel (verso type) (5)
(2) Hooped barrel (bombard type) (3)

21. Breech Chambers (various sizes and styles (Total 30)
(1) Iron (29)
(2) Bronze (1)

22. Breech Chamber Parts
(1) Handles and fragments
(2) Wooden plugs

23. Breech Chamber Parts (Total 43)
(1) Handles and Fragments (17)
(2) Wooden plugs (10)
(3) Fiber touch hole plugs (3)
(4) Powder samples (12)
(5) Fiber wad (1)

24. Iron Breech Wedges (Forelocks) (8)

25. Cannon Balls (Total 67)
(1) Stone (5)
(2) Lead (10)
(3) Lead covered iron (27)
(4) Iron (two fragmentary) (25)

26. Small Round Shot (Musket or Grape Shot) (Total 30)
(1) Lead (1)
(2) Lead Covered Iron (1)
(3) Iron (1)

27. Crossbows (4)
(1) Bow and most of stock present (1)
(2) Bow and part of stock present (1)
(3) Stock fragment (1)
(4) Bow with no stock (1)

28. Navigational Astrolabes (Total 3)
(1) Alidade present but bent (2)
(2) Alidade missing (1)

29. Miscellaneous Iron Objects (96)
(1) Gudgeon bar for rudder (1)
(2) Half an anchor fluke (1)
(3) Sledge hammer head (1)
(4) Part hammer head (1)
(5) Chains and chain fragments (some attached eye bolts) (11)
(6) Spikes, bolts, nails, pins, (including fragments) (53)
(7) L shaped tools, caulking tools (3)
(8) Small L - shaped wire object (1)
(9) Strap fragments (8)
(10) Small shackles or hoops (2)
(11) Knife or sword blade fragments (2)
(12) Small rings, possibly clinch rings (1)
(13) Circular piece with pin (7)

30. Lead Objects (593)
(1) Sounding weights (3)
(2) Small weights (10)
(3) Bar with shipping mark (1)
(4) Bars, no marks (2).
(5) Small wedge (1)
(6) Ingots, chunks, irregular pieces (1)
(7) Sheeting or patching scraps, some with nail holes (570)

31. Objects of Other Metal (Total 9)
(1) Curved rod shaped piece, tin alloy (1)
(2) Encrusted fragment of spoon (pewter) (1)
(3) Button fragment (1)
(4) Fragments of pewter utensil (3)
(5) Small unidentified slivers (3)

32. Miscellaneous Stone Objects (Total 281)
(1) Ballast (240)
(2) Rock (may be ballast) (31)
(3) Slate (10)

33. Miscellaneous Organic Objects (Total 48)
(1) Rope and fiber fragments (22)
(2) Bits of wood and rope from around spikes and cannon ball (5)
(3) Miscellaneous wood (18)
(4) Seed (1)
(5) Canvas, possible hair, hide attached (1)
(6) Cloth fragment (1)

34. Encrustations with Molds or Oxidized Metal (Total 421)

35. Bone and Shell (Total 16)
(1) Possible domestic animals (5)
(2) Shellfish remains (11)

Artifact List per Texas

The following artifacts were recovered from the *San Esteban* shipwreck recovered by The State of Texas. The control number for the shipwreck is 41 KN 10.

1. Coins (Total 362)
(1) 1 - real silver, Carlos and Johanna, Mexico City Mint (1)
(2) 2 - real, silver, Carlos and Johanna, Mexico City Mint (114)
(3) 4 - real, silver, Carlos and Johanna, Mexico City Mint (209)
(4) Santo Domingo Mint
(a) Copper coin - 4 maravedis (1)
(b) 4 - real, silver, Carlos and Johanna, F assayer (2)
(5) 1 - real, silver, Ferdinand & Isabella, Seville Mint (1)
(6) - unidentified fragments, silver (34)

2. Silver Disks (ingots) (Total 37)
(1) Large (1)
(2) Medium (3)
(3) Small (15)
(4) Irregular pieces and disk fragments (18)

3. Gold Bar (1)

4. Cannons, Wrought Iron (total 4)
(1) Swivel (verso) (1)
(2) Hooped barrel (bombard) (3)

5. Breach Chambers, Wrought Iron (Total 32)
(1) For swivel (verso) (17)
(2) For hooped barrel (bombard) (15)

6. Associated Parts for Wrought Iron Cannons (Total 29)
(1) Iron breech wedge (forelock) fragments (2)
(2) Wooden plugs for breech chambers (12)
(3) Gun powder samples (9)
(4) Fiber touch-hole plugs (3)
(5) Hooped barrel (bombard carriage) (2)
(6) Cone-shaped object – possibly a verso swivel mount part (1)

7. Cannon Balls (Total 68)
(1) Stone (1)
(2) Lead (1)
(3) Lead - covered iron (28)
(4) Iron (38)

8. Small Shot (Total 5)
(1) Lead (4)
(2) Dice of iron or core of lead-covered iron shot (1)

9. Crossbow Part (Total 1)
(1) Goat's foot lever claw frame (1)

10. Miscellaneous Copper Alloy Objects (Total 40)
(1) Divider fragments (2)
(2) Set screw (possibly from a cross-staff or similar instrument) (1)
(3) Wire link (1)
(4) Scale weight (1)
(5) Straight pins (25)
(6) Sheath for straight pins (1)
(7) Buckle (1)
(8) Ring (1)
(9) Tacks – possibly decorative (3)
(10) Small fragments (4)

11. Pewter Porringers (2)

12. Anchors and Anchor Parts, Wrought Iron (Total 13)
(1) Anchors (7)
(2) Anchor Ring Fragments (4 oxidized) (5)
(3) Arm and fluke fragments (1)

13. Rudder Fittings, Wrought Iron (Total 6)
(1) Gudgeon (1)
(2) Pintles (2)
(3) Gudgeon or pintle strap fragments (3)

14. Tools (Total 6)
(1) Small auger or reamer, wrought iron
(2) Auger, wrought iron (1)
(3) Pincers, wrought iron (1)
(4) Pick adze, wrought iron (1)
(5) Thumble like object, wrought iron (1)
(6) Awl, bone (1)

15. Miscellaneous Wrought Iron Objects (Total 365)
(1) Forelock bolts (4 oxidized) (15)
(2) Spikes, nails, and tacks (many oxidized) (172)
(3) Shear hook (1)
(4) Case knife with brass foil and pin (1)
(5) Clinch rings (8)
(6) Forelock (wedge for forelock bolt) (1)
(7) Chains (standing rigging; 4 oxidized) (5)
(8) Small chain with staples (1)
(9) Miscellaneous chain links (3 oxidized) (7)
(10) Strap hinge (1)
(11) Ring with hinge attachment (1)
(12) Straps or barrel hoops (149)
(13) Bar stock (6)

16. Lead Objects Total 96)
(1) Bar (1)
(2) Sounding weights (2)
(3) Small weights (6)
(4) Straps (54)
(5) Scraps, fragments, slivers (33)

17. Organic Material (Total 132)
(1) Keel section with sternpost and gudgeon (1)
(2) Beam, plank, and other wood fragments (13)
(3) Cargo container fragments (10)
(4) Miscellaneous wood fragments (4
(5) Hemp gaskets and caulking (9)
(6) Rope (24)
(7) Hair samples (2)
(8) Resin (1)
(9) Cloth fragments (20)
(10) Provision remains, including bones, nutshells, horn, seeds, olive
pits (39)
(11) Cockroaches (9)

18. Ceramics and Glass (Total 170)
(1) Plain potsherds (110)
(2) Glazed potsherds (52)
(3) Brick fragments (3)
(4) Glass bottle base (1)
(5) Glass sherds (4)

19. Jewelry (Total 2)
(1) Wooden cross with sheet and wire goal (1)
(2) Square quartz bead (1)

20. Aboriginal Objects (Total 6)
(1) Polished pyrite hemisphere (1)
(2) Obsidian blades (4)
(3) Iron pyrite bead (1)

21. Ballast Stones (thousands)

The number of total objects in all categories was 1,446

Reference Resources

Alperin, Lynn (1977) Custodians of the Coast: History of the U.S. Corps of Engineers at Galveston. U.S. Government Printing Office, Washington D.C.

Anderson, R.G.W. (1972) The Mariners Astrolabe. Catalogue of an Exhibition at the Royal Scottish Museum, 19 August – 29 September, 1972.

Arnold Barto (1986) The Platoro Lawsuit: the final chapter. In Proceedings of the Sixteenth Conference on Underwater Archaeology, edited by Paul F. Johnson, pp. 1-8. The Society for Historical Archaeology, Special Publication Series, Number 4.

.... (1978) Underwater (1977) Site Test Excavations Off Padre Island, Texas. Texas Antiquities Committee, Publication # 5. Austin.

.... (1976) An Underwater Archaeological Magnetometer Survey and Site Test Excavation Project off Padre Island, Texas. Texas Antiquities Committee, Publication # 3. Austin.

Arnold, J. Barto and Larry V. Norby (1987) Preliminary Report on the Padre Island Archaeological Survey for 1986. Paper presented to the 1987 Society for Historical Archaeology Conference on Historical and Underwater Archaeology. Savannah Georgia,
Bascom, Willard (1980) Winds and Beaches. Garden City, New York: Anchor Books.

Bass, George F, Ed (1972) A History of Seafaring Based on Underwater Archaeology. London: Thames & Hudson.

Burgess, R. F., and Carl J. Clausen. (1976) Gold galleons and Archaeology: A History of the Spanish 1715 Plate Fleet and the True Story of the Great Florida Treasure Find. Indianapolis.

Castaneda, Carlos E. (1936) The Dominican Martyrs of Texas, 1553 – 1554, in Our Catholic Heritage in Texas, Seven vols, Chapter. V, pp. 140-156, Austin: Von Boeckmann Jones Co.

Chapelle, Howard I. (1982) The History of American Sailing Ships. New York.

Cipolla, Carlo M. (1965) Guns, Sails and Empires: Technological Innovation and the Early Phases of European Expansion 1400-1700. New York: Minerva Press.

Clausen, Carl J. 'A Spanish Treasure Ship'. Contributions of the Florida State Museum, XII (1965), 1 – 48.

Clayton, Lawrence A. 'Trade and Navigation in the Seventeenth Century Viceroyalty of Peru'. Journal of Latin American Studies, VII (1975), 1-21.

Curray, J (1960) Sediments and history of Holocene transgressions, continental shelf, northwest Gulf of Mexico, a symposium summarizing the results of work carried on in Project 51 of the American Petroleum Institute, 1951-1958.

Davis, Charles G. (1984) American Sailing Ships: Their Plans and History. New York.

Degan, Kathleen A. Artifacts of the Spanish Colonies of Florida and the Caribbean, 1500-1800. Vol I, Ceramics, Glassware and Beads. Washington D.C., 1987.

Dowman, Elizabeth A. (1970) Conservation in Field Archaeology. London: Methuen & Co, Ltd.

Earl, Peter. (1980) The Treasure of the Conception: The Wreck of the Almiranta. New York.

Espey Huston & Associates, Inc. (EH&A) (1988) Draft Environmental Impact Statement (EIS), Port Mansfield Entrance Channel: Ocean Dredged Material Disposal Site Designation. Prepared for the Galveston District Corps of Engineers. October 1988, Austin.

Foulkes, Charles (1967) The Armourer and his Craft. New York: Benjamin Blom.

Goggin, John M. (1964) The Spanish Olive Jar. Coral Gables: University of Miami Press.

Hamilton, D.L. (1976) Conservation of metal objects from underwater sites: A study in methods. Texas Memorial Museum, Miscellaneous Papers Number 4 and The Texas Antiquities Committee, Publication Number 1, A Joint Publication. Austin Texas.

Hale, John R. (1966) Age of Exploration. New York: Time Inc.

Hamilton, Earl J. (1929) Imports of Gold and Silver into Spain. Quarterly Journal of Economics. Vol XXXVII, pp. 430-450.

Haring, Clarence Henry (1964) Trade and Navigation between Spain and the Indies in the Time of the Hapsburgs. Cambridge: Harvard University Press.

Hays, T.R. and Eugene Herrin (1970) Padre Island Project. Report to the Texas Antiquities Committee. Institute for Underwater Research, Inc. Dallas.

Hatseed, Henry (1920) Early Breech Loading Guns. The Mariners Mirror, Vol 6, No. 1 (Jan), pp. 120-121.

Henry, W.K., D.M. Driscoll and J.P. McCormack (1975) Hurricanes on the Texas Coast: Description and climatology.Texas A&M University Publication No. TAMU-SG-75-501.

Hime, Henry W. L. (1915) The Origin of Artillery. London: Longmans. Hoffman, Paul E. (1980) The Spanish Crown and the Defense of the Caribbean, 1535 – 1585. Baton Rouge: Louisiana State University Press.

Horner, David (1971) The Treasure Galleons: Clues to Millions in Sunken Gold and Silver. New York: Dodd Mead & Co.

Johnston, Paul F. 'Treasure salvage, Archaeological Ethics, and Maritime Museums.' International Journal of Nautical Archaeology, XXII (1993), 53-60.

Landstrom, Bjorn (1961) The Ship. London: Allen & Unwin. Lewis, Michael (1936) The Guns of the Jesus of Lubeck. Vol XXII, No, 3 (July), pp. 324-325.

Lyon, Eugene. 'The Trouble with Treasure.' National Geographic Magazine, CLI (1976), 787-809.

Mahan, William (1967) Padre Island: Treasure Kingdom of the World. Waco: Texian Press.

Manucy, Albert (1949) Artillery Through The Ages: A Short Illustrated History of Cannons Emphasizing Types Used in America. Washington D.C., National Park Service.

Marx, Robert F. (1968) The Treasure Fleets of the Spanish Main. Cleveland: World Publishing Company.

.... (1971) Shipwrecks of the Western Hemisphere 1492-1825. New York: World Publishing Company.

McDonald, David and J. Barto Arnold III (1979) Documentary Sources for the Wreck of the New Spain Fleet of 1554. Texas Antiquities Committee, Publication # 8, Austin.

McNickle, A.J.S. (1962) Spanish Colonial Coins of North America, Mexico Mint. Mexico City: Sociedad Numismatica de Mexico.

Morton. R.A. and M.J. Pieper (1977) Shoreline changes on central Padre Island (Yarborough Pass to Mansfield Channel): An analysis of historical changes of the Texas Gulf shoreline. University of Texas, Bureau of Economic Geology, Circular 77-2.

Nordby, Larry V. and J. Barto Arnold III (1986) The Padre Island National Seashore Archaeological Project of 1985. Paper presented to the Seventeenth Conference on Underwater Archaeology. Sacramento California.

Ojos, Alonso (1554) Homebound register of the ship Nuestra Senora *Santa Maria de Yciar*. Archivo General de Indias, Contrataacion 2490 and 1788, Sevilla, Spain.

Olds, Doris L. (1976) Texas Legacy from the Gulf: A report on 16th Century Shipwreck Materials from the Texas Tidelands. Texas Memorial Museum, Miscellaneous Papers # 5. Texas Antiquities Committee, Publication # 2. Austin.

Pearson, Charles E. & Hoffman, Paul E. (1995) The Last Voyage of the El Nuevo Constante: The Wreck and Recovery of an Eighteenth-Century Spanish Ship Off the Louisiana Coast. Baton Rouge: Louisiana State University Press.

Philips, Carla Rahn. (1986) Six Galleons for the King of Spain: Imperial Defense in the Early Eighteenth Century. Baltimore: John Hopkins Press.

Steel, David. (1977) The Elements and Practice of Naval Architecture (2 Volumes) London: Guild Hall Press.

INDEX

Vessel Index

Alphabetic Index

A